MARY KAY

Mary Kay

Mary Kay Ash

Third Edition

HarperPerennial
A Division of HarperCollinsPublishers

HarperCollins books may be purchased for educational, business, or sales promotional use. For information please write: Special Markets Department, HarperCollins Publishers, Inc., 10 East 53rd Street, New York, NY 10022.

FIRST EDITION

ISBN 0-06-092601-5

96 97 98   RRD(H)   20 19 18 17 16 15 14 13

Dedicated to the thousands of women who
DARED
to step out of their "comfort zones" and
USE
their God-given talents and abilities,
realizing that God did not have time
to make a nobody—
just a
SOMEBODY!

Contents

Photographs follow pages 48 and 128

Acknowledgments

I would like to gratefully acknowledge the contributions of three special people who provided invaluable assistance in preparing this manuscript. First, thanks to Bob Shook for his sincere words of encouragement and his amazing power of organization. And to Linda Perigo Moore, a successful author in her own right, and to Yvonne Pendleton, of our Mary Kay staff, who helped assemble all the needed information for the epilogue—thanks for helping me tell my story in exactly the right words. Without them, this book would probably never have been written.

Preface

I started to write a book once before—shortly after retiring from a twenty-five-year career in direct sales. My retirement was less than a week old, and I already knew why so many obituaries include the phrase "He retired last year." In fact, I lived across the street from a mortuary, and I began to wonder if I should just call them up and tell them to "come on over."

Building my career and caring for my family had been *everything* to me. I never liked those things other people seemed to enjoy for relaxation. For example, I never had time to learn how to play games like tennis, and I absolutely *hated* cocktail parties. To me, work and growth were the same. And without my work, I found that I had no reason to get out of bed each morning.

Thus, after retirement, the only thing left for me to do was to think back over those active, productive years. During my career I had faced and solved many problems that are unique to women in business. Much of the time I was actually handicapped or held back by outdated ideas of what a woman should and should not do when working with men. "Maybe," I thought, "just maybe, I could use my experience to help other women over these same hurdles." That's when I decided to organize my thoughts by writing down all the lessons I had learned. When I began this exercise I was filled with memories of opportunities denied me because I was a woman. And I hoped that making my list would clear my heart of bitterness. It did. But just as important was the realization that I had compiled a list of factors that defined the "dream company." In this abstract company, relationships would be based upon the golden rule, and women would be allowed to pursue unlimited opportunities. No one would be held back if she had the skills and determination to succeed.

I used the notes to begin what I intended as a management training book. But before long, I asked myself, "Why are you *theorizing* about a dream company? Why don't you just start one?" Mary Kay Cosmetics was founded on Friday, September 13, 1963. And through the ensuing decades it has been my joy and honor to watch it grow. With the help of God and my wonderful family, friends, and associates, we have evolved from a little storefront company with nine saleswomen to an international family of hundreds of thousands of Beauty Consultants—each controlling her own independent business. The solutions I listed so long ago have given thousands and thousands of women the opportunity to become so much more than they ever thought they could be.

But I'm not stopping there. Nothing wilts faster than a laurel rested upon, and so we have always worked to maintain the very best products and to practice the most sophisticated management techniques available. It was with this in mind that we made the decision, in 1968, to open ownership in Mary Kay Cosmetics, Inc., and to become listed on the public stock exchange. At the time, it was an important stepping-stone for us, but as the years passed circumstances changed. We came to believe that our corporate growth would be impeded if we continued along this route.

In the spring of 1985, we decided that it would be in the best interest of our people and our customers if we got out of the stock market. So, basing our decision on objective and independent expert opinions, we made fair-value offers to buy back all outstanding public shares of Mary Kay Cosmetics and return to a family corporation.

The advantages of such a move are many. Most important, we are not adversely affected as investors buy and sell in an ever-fluctuating stock market.

One important thing has not changed since we came off the stock market—every Consultant and Director associated with us still maintains her own *independent* business—that's the way it's always been. But at our corporate headquarters, we can more closely monitor and ensure those basic principles upon which our company was built.

As founder and chairman emeritus of Mary Kay Cosmetics, I've received quite a lot of publicity. Now when I have something to say, people seem to listen. It's not that I'm saying anything different from what I've said all my life. But apparently, when a person achieves some success, what he or she has to say becomes more "important." So here I am writing that book again.

I've never been one to pass up an opportunity. As often as I can, you'll hear me talking about the many wonderful opportunities in this world for women. And while some of my philosophy is old-fashioned—employing the golden rule and living something we have come to call the "Go-Give" spirit—it's also a "Yes, you can!" philosophy which I think is very much in tune with *today's woman*. Not only that, but it works.

I want to share with you now my philosophies, my inner feelings, my disappointments, and my joys. You will probably notice that I don't give too many dates. Of course, I remember dates like my children's birthdays. I'm a woman, and what woman isn't sentimental about those things? But if you had just a few dates and were even slightly good at arithmetic, you'd know my age. And I *never* tell my age. Why should I? I believe that a woman who will tell her age will tell *anything*. All I'll tell you is that I'm not as old as some people seem to think. (I've heard the rumors!) The best thing I ever heard on the subject is this: If you really didn't know your exact age, how old would you say that you were? I feel twenty-four!

This book is for anyone who feels young and who wishes to succeed. You see, God didn't have time to make a "nobody." As a result, you can have, or be, anything you want. Every one of us is important and necessary to God's plan. If someone else will just believe in you—you will be able to do *great* things. I know this because someone once believed in me. At a time when I may not have displayed much in the way of experience or skill, someone believed that I could succeed. And largely because of this confidence, I did!

MARY KAY

1

You Can Do It!

THERE ARE FOUR KINDS of people in this world:

- those who make things happen
- those who watch things happen
- those who wonder what happened
- those who don't know that *anything* happened!

I knew from a very early age that I wanted to be first on that list. And in the years since, I have learned that people who do succeed are set apart by their personalities, objectives, and abilities. Specifically this means that they have

- enthusiasm (with purpose)
- discipline
- willingness (to work, to serve, and to learn)
- determination
- appreciation of others

I said that I learned this lesson; I did not say that it came easily or dropped into my lap. When I was seven years old, my daddy came home from the sanatorium; and although three years' treatment had arrested his tuberculosis, he was not completely cured. During the rest of my childhood, he remained an invalid and in need of a great deal of tender loving care.

For all those years, my mother was the sole support of our family. She had been trained as a nurse, but eventually found work as the manager of a restaurant in Houston. The job didn't pay as well as such jobs do today, and the salary was undoubtedly lower because she was a woman. Mother worked fourteen hours a day, leaving home each morning at five (before I awoke) and returning at nine at night (often after I was asleep). My older brother and sister were grown and gone, so it became my responsibility to take care of my daddy.

It never occurred to me that things should be any different. I would come home from school and clean the house. Then I would do my homework. But I accepted this, and what's more, I enjoyed it. Even though some of my duties were supposed to be too difficult for a child, nobody ever told me that. As a result, I just *did* them.

Still, preparing meals was often a great challenge. My mother was a marvelous cook, but the job became mine when she couldn't be home in time to make our family dinner. At the tender age of seven, I could hardly be considered a master chef. (Remember, there were no such things as frozen dinners or fast-food carry-outs.) If Daddy wanted chili or chicken for dinner and I didn't know how to cook it, I would call my mother. During those days, I rarely had the opportunity to learn anything from her in person—she just couldn't be there to teach me. But how often I have said since then, "Thank God for the telephone!" It became my lifeline and my primary contact with my mother. Whenever I called her, she found a way to make time for me and to patiently explain what I had to do.

"Mother? Hi! Daddy wants potato soup tonight."

"Potato soup? Okay, honey. First get out the big pot, the one you used yesterday. Then you take two potatoes . . ."

She'd go through every step, one at a time, trying to think of everything I would need to know. I hadn't been raised to be a complainer, but I'm sure she knew that my job sometimes seemed overwhelming. Because when she was through with her instructions, she always added, "Honey, *you can do it.*"

Our family situation meant that I had to do many things that most children weren't expected to do. For instance, if I needed new clothing, I had to go by myself to downtown Houston. I took these Saturday trips alone, because my best friend was not allowed to travel on the streetcar without an adult. After all, we were just seven years old.

Don't forget—these were the days when a little girl's dress was sixty-nine cents and eggs were nineteen cents a dozen. Mother would give me perhaps $1.50, and I would go pick out a dress or blouse. I loved doing this—it was the highlight of my week. The only problem I had was convincing the clerks that I really was allowed to make such decisions. Sometimes it was enough to show them the money, but often they would demand, "Where's your mother?" Then I would explain our circumstances, give them the phone number for Mother's restaurant and tell them, "You can call her. She'll tell you it's okay."

After shopping, I got to go to Kress's for a pimento-cheese sandwich on toast and a Coke. Then I'd go to a movie. I lived for these afternoons "on the town." I think the meal was usually twenty cents and the show was about a dime, so for thirty cents I had a wow of an afternoon.

When I first began these excursions, I was a little anxious about catching the right streetcar and finding my way around. Then I remembered my mother saying, "You can do it, honey." I must have heard those words a thousand times, and she always said them with total conviction. Now I realize that she must have been very anxious about the responsibilities I had to assume. But you would never have known it to hear her. As far as I was concerned, my mother *knew* I could do it. Her words became the theme of my childhood. They have stayed with me all my life: "You can do it."

The confidence my mother instilled has served me throughout my adult life. Without it, Mary Kay Cosmetics might have
fizzled before it even began. It was 1963. After twenty-five
years as a professional saleswoman, with my children grown,
I just decided that retirement did not suit me. And so I had
developed a strategy and philosophy for beginning my own
"dream company." I had recruited several salespeople and
invested my life savings into the chance of a lifetime. Using
my years of experience in direct sales, I was going to train and
supervise the Beauty Consultants, while my husband was
going to handle the administrative details of our new business. We had assembled boxes of bottles and jars and brand-
new labels that read, "Beauty by Mary Kay." (Of course, this
was later changed to Mary Kay Cosmetics.)

Exactly one month before we were scheduled to open, my
husband and I were having breakfast together. He was reading the final percentage figures for our company, and I was
listening very much as a wife often does when her husband
talks about the budget—with half an ear, because I considered
it to be "his problem." At that moment, he suffered a fatal
heart attack.

I believe that work is often the best antidote for grief. And
so, despite my shock, I decided to open the business as
planned. Starting the company had been my dream and my
idea, but I had never imagined that I would run it alone. I
knew that I didn't have the needed administrative skills; and
yet, at this point, all the merchandise, bottles, and labels were
useless if the company folded. I *had* to go on.

I turned to both my attorney and my accountant for
advice.

"Mary Kay," my attorney said, shaking his head, "liqui-
date the business right now and recoup whatever cash you
can. If you don't, you'll end up penniless."

I had hoped that my accountant would be a little more
encouraging, but after studying the situation he said, "You

can't possibly do it. This commission schedule will never work. It's just a matter of time before the company goes bankrupt—and you along with it."

The day of my husband's funeral, my sons and my daughter came to Dallas from Houston. Perhaps it was the worst possible time to make a business decision, but it could no longer be delayed. After the funeral, we sat in my living room and discussed the recommendations I had received. My children listened in silence.

My twenty-year-old son, Richard, was a sales representative for Prudential Life Insurance Company. One of the youngest agents in Texas, he was making the incredible salary of $480 a month. (I thought that was just unbelievable—after all, he was just a kid!) If Mary Kay were to become a reality, I needed his help; but there was no way that I could afford a salary like that. I took a deep breath and offered him $250 a month to help me guide the new company. Richard accepted without hesitation. And over the horrified protests of other family members and friends, he immediately quit his job and moved to Dallas.

My elder son, Ben, was twenty-seven years old, married and the father of two. He could not pull up roots and move as quickly as his brother. But after hearing my plans to continue the company, he said, "One day I'd like to join you and Richard." Then calmly and deliberately he reached into his breast pocket and pulled out a savings passbook. The balance showed $4,500—a sum I knew represented everything he had saved since high school.

"Mother," he said. "I think you could do anything in this world that you wanted to." Then he handed me the passbook. "Here's my savings. If it will help you in any way, I want you to have it."

Eight months later—when we needed someone to handle our expanding warehouse—Ben left his job with a Houston welding company and moved his family to Dallas. At that time, he gave up a salary of $750 a month, and started with the company at the same pay as Richard—$250 a month. And still later, my daughter, Marylyn, joined us and became the first Mary Kay Director in Houston.

On Friday, September 13, 1963, one month after the funeral, Mary Kay Cosmetics opened on schedule. With myself, nine salespeople, and my twenty-year-old son as financial administrator, how did I know that I could do it? Well, I didn't! I had no crystal ball. All I knew was that I *had* to do it. As for the predictions of my attorney and accountant, I figured they didn't have any crystal balls either. Besides, they didn't understand the business the way I did. I also knew that I would never have a second chance to put my dream into action. If Mary Kay Cosmetics failed, I wasn't going back into an easy retirement. I'd be broke! And that meant that I'd have to work for someone else for the rest of my life. That's a very strong incentive! So no matter what anyone thought, I would not give up my dream. My children had said, "You can do it." And that was all I needed.

Of course, my children had grown up believing their mother could do just about anything. I had been virtually their sole emotional and financial support from the day of their birth to the day they were grown and on their own. They had watched me get up at five every morning to catch up on my work, get them off to school, and then go out to earn our living in sales. They knew that I was always there from the time they got home until after dinner, when I left again to work. Over the years, the family had moved to nicer houses and better neighborhoods, and my children knew that I had somehow managed that.

Richard and Ben knew what my advisers had said. And yet they had given their unqualified support. I never needed that kind of support more desperately than I did on the day of the funeral; it reassured me and filled me with new confidence.

"Mother," Richard had gently said as he put his arm around my shoulders, "Ben and I have talked about this. All our lives, we've watched you make a success out of everything you've done. If you could be successful working for someone else, we know you can do even better working for yourself."

It's just possible that at the time the boys had a little more confidence in the Mary Kay dream than Mary Kay did! I knew my way around in direct sales; and I knew the ideas I had built into my company were good and just. But a company administered by a twenty-year-old boy? Only yesterday Richard had been a teenager, wanting nothing more than a motorcycle! Yes, he had been a good student, but help me successfully operate a business? I honestly couldn't see Richard replacing my late husband in that role. I told myself, "It will be a miracle."

But I had mistrusted God. I should have known that when God closes a door, He always opens a window. I might not have realized how much ability Richard had, but God did. He had prepared Richard and placed him in a position to help me build our company. Five years after we opened, Richard was given the Man of the Year Award by the American Marketing Association. At that time, he was the youngest man ever to have received the honor. Later, when Mary Kay Cosmetics became a public corporation, Richard was one of the youngest people ever to be president of a company listed on the New York Stock Exchange. From the very beginning, Richard was a godsend. He ran all administrative aspects of our business, from manufacturing to marketing, leaving me free to spend my full time and energies on directing and motivating the sales organization. We were quite a team—and still are. I depend on his financial expertise more and more each day. In fact, he even balances my personal checkbook.

Even with the vital support of my sons, many others were telling me that my dream would never work. All the odds seemed against us. But memories of my mother's belief in me kept running through my mind. Whenever the task seemed most impossible, I would simply repeat those words she had instilled in me for all those years, "You can do it, Mary Kay. You can *do* it!"

Still, I'm not certain that any *person* can take total credit for the success of my dream. A friend of mine once said, "Mary Kay Cosmetics was a divine accident looking for a place to happen." And I think this is correct. In 1963, the social forces that now support the financial and legal equality of women had not gained public favor. And yet, here was a company that would give women all the opportunities I had never had. I don't think God wanted a world in which a woman would have to work fourteen hours a day to support her family, as my mother had done. I believe He used this company as a vehicle to give women a chance. And I feel very humble and very fortunate to have had a part in showing other women the way.

"You can do it!" is an everyday motto at Mary Kay Cosmetics. And so often a woman will join us who is in desperate need of hearing this message. Frequently she is a homemaker who has been out of the job market for years. Perhaps she *never* worked outside the home; and now, because of divorce or widowhood, she finds herself seeking a career. Maybe she worked long and hard in another field, never having heard those words of encouragement. For whatever the reason, she often needs to build her feelings of self-esteem and worth.

Obviously she must first be told, "You can do it!" But we can't stop there, and we don't. The basic philosophies upon which our company is founded assure this woman that she will be carefully guided along every step of her professional development. Following the golden rule, every Consultant and Director will gladly share experience and enthusiasm until she reaches her full potential. And as she becomes more efficient at setting and meeting career goals, she will become more confident in *every way*. That's why if you ask a Mary Kay Consultant about her career, she will probably tell you that it has become a way of life—not just a way of earning money.

Of course, we don't take the credit for her success. When a shy or inexperienced Consultant evolves into a top sales professional, *she's* the one who did it. All we did was provide some needed guidance and encouragement. You see, her talent was always there—she just may not have been aware of it.

Sadly, most people live and die with their music still unplayed. They never dare to try. Why? Because they lack self-confidence. Women, especially, have *so much* potential they never tap. For example, Grandma Moses didn't begin painting until she was seventy-eight years old. When asked why, she said that she just never tried. And yet in only four years, her works were exhibited at the Metropolitan Museum of Art. I can't help but wonder how much more the world would have seen of her beautiful art if she had only started earlier!

For me, seeing so many women grow and develop has been the most meaningful accomplishment of Mary Kay Cosmetics. Everyone benefits when we all pass on the "You can do it!" spirit. Often we meet a woman when she is like a tight little rosebud, full of potential never revealed. After a few months of praise and encouragement, she blossoms into a beautiful rose, poised and confident in her newfound skills.

At a recent meeting, I heard a Consultant say, "When I started with Mary Kay, I was terrified to speak in front of six people. I didn't see how I was going to make it through my first skin-care class." That same woman was making this remark—on stage, smiling and radiant—before eight thousand people. I think it's obvious that someone did a very good job of telling her, "You can do it!"

If you ever come to visit Mary Kay headquarters in Dallas, you may see someone wearing a diamond pin in the shape of a bumblebee. Be assured that she is one of our top performers. Within our organization, the bumblebee has become the ultimate symbol of accomplishment. We selected it because of what the bumblebee represents for all women. You see, years ago, aerodynamic engineers studied this creature and decided that it simply *should not be able* to fly! Its wings are too weak and its body too heavy for flight. Everything seems to tell the bumblebee, "You'll never get off the ground." But I like to think that maybe—just maybe—our Divine Creator whispered, "You can do it!" so it did!

2

A Competitive Spirit

COMPETITION CAN BE a very strong motivation. But I have learned that it becomes most powerful when you compete with yourself and when you learn from your failures.

As I was growing up, my mother constantly told me, "Anything anyone else can do, you can do better!" After hearing this enough times, I became convinced that I *could* do better. And in my mother's eyes, one way for me to prove this was by making straight As in school—Bs just weren't good enough. I didn't want to disappoint her or myself, and so I worked as hard as I could to reach the goals she had set for me. But as I worked to make the best grades in my class, I found that competition and doing my best became my goals, too. During those days, I never thought in terms of *beating* the other children; all I really wanted to do was to better my own best achievements. Soon it became necessary for me to excel in anything I did! Yes, I wanted to sell the most tickets for the May Fete or the most boxes of Girl Scout cookies; but more important, I wanted to sell more tickets or more cookies than I had the previous year.

As I progressed through my career, the competitive spirit my mother had encouraged helped me through some very difficult days. And with each challenge, I concentrated upon competing with myself. Every Saturday I computed my weekly sales, and I always wanted my earnings to be a little more than the week before. When I was successful, it wasn't because I was more talented than the next salesperson; I was just willing to make more sacrifices. I was willing to work hard and pay the price for that success.

Of course I didn't always reach my goal, but fortunately, my mother also taught me how to lose. She did this by encouraging me to look to the future: to do better the next time—to try harder. I think it's extremely important for young people to learn that "you can't win 'em all." It is simply impossible to be *the best* all the time. Today when I see parents pushing children to win (as they often do in some Little League teams), I just pray that someone is also teaching those youngsters how to accept defeat. Because anyone who competes has to face defeat and learn how to go on from there.

One of my favorite expressions is "We fail forward to success." It's true—we learn from our failures. And how many times have we all heard it said that the person who never fails never attempts anything? I've found that successful people are never afraid to try, because they are never afraid to fail. Many times I have told the people in our organization, "If we ever decide to compare knees, you're going to find that I have more scars than anyone in the room. That's because I have fallen down and gotten up so many times in my life."

During the early years of Mary Kay Cosmetics, we didn't always set the world on fire. The company you see today was created in spite of many disappointments and setbacks. But I envisioned a company in which any woman could compete against her own best effort and thus become as successful as she wanted. From the very beginning, the doors of our company were open wide for any woman who believed that hard work and determination could conquer failures—any woman who had the courage to dream and who was willing to pay the price.

I believe you can have anything you want in this world,

but yes, you do have to pay a price. Throughout my childhood I knew that in order to get something, I had to give up something else. When I was a student, that usually meant giving up an extra hour or two of sleep so I could study. When I began my sales career, it meant giving up even more sleep so that I could do my housework and care for my children. As a young working mother it also meant giving up my social life. There weren't enough hours in the day to work, keep house, look after the children, and have time left over for anything else. But I never resented these sacrifices. I wanted to support my family well, to buy a nicer house, and to move to a nicer neighborhood. I knew that each of these goals had a price, and my spirit of competition is what always helped me feel that the price was worth it.

Competing and striving to excel can also be a lot of fun! As a young child, I enjoyed the satisfaction of bringing home the As my mother expected. And in junior high school, I experienced more of the fun of competition when I discovered three new talents: typing, extemporaneous speaking, and debating.

Typing was my first challenge. My teacher, Mrs. Davis, took me under her wing; and with her encouragement, I was determined to become the best typist that I could. My greatest wish at that time was to have a typewriter of my own, but I knew it would be very expensive, and so it never occurred to me to ask for one. Then, almost as in a miracle, my mother surprised me with a Woodstock typewriter. To this day, I can't imagine how she was able to save enough money for the down payment or how long it must have taken her to pay for that wonderful machine. But it was so like her to find a way. She always went to extraordinary lengths to encourage me to excel in whatever I did, and she realized that having my own typewriter would help me develop my typing skills. Needless to say, that old Woodstock was one of my most prized possessions. And knowing what my mother must have sacrificed to pay for it made me even more determined to become an expert typist. I cannot describe my satisfaction when, at long last, I brought home a trophy for being the best typist in my class.

Another ambition at that young age was to be a good extemporaneous speaker. And as in typing, a wonderful teacher encouraged and coached me. Before I was out of junior high, I had competed in a statewide contest and had actually placed second. What a thrill it was for me to feel that I was the second best speaker in the entire state of Texas! In high school I became interested in formal debate, and after making the team, I also won some honors in that field. These youthful accomplishments gave me the courage to practice and improve my speaking skills. I still work hard to perfect each line of every speech I am asked to give. And as a result, speaking before thousands of women at Mary Kay meetings still gives me the same challenge and thrill that I got back then in speech competitions. In fact, the thrill is even bigger!

Encouragement from my mother and teachers was extremely important to me, but as I look back on my childhood, I suspect that the biggest influence on my competitive spirit was my friendship with Dorothy Zapp. When we were children, I simply enjoyed our special relationship, but now I realize that being Dorothy's friend exposed me to an exciting new world. Subconsciously I must have recognized that I could earn a place in such a world if I were only willing to work for it.

Dorothy's family was much better off financially than my own, and while she lived just around the corner, her house was by far the nicest one in our neighborhood. Every day Dorothy wore a crisp, starched pinafore to school. (Remember, that was before the days of wash and wear.) Every morning her mother curled her long golden hair until she looked as if she had just stepped from the cover of a magazine. And every morning, clean but plain little Mary Kathlyn would appear on the front porch to walk to school with picture-perfect Dorothy.

I still blame those mornings at Dorothy's house for the fact that I've always been somewhat on the plump side. Dorothy was a tiny, fragile child who never wanted to eat her breakfast. Her mother would coax her to eat her toast with strawberry jam and drink her glass of milk with ice. But when her mother wasn't looking, Dorothy would pass them over to me. And who was I to see that good food go to waste? After all, Dorothy's breakfast was sumptuous fare compared to the bowl of cereal I had fixed for my own morning meal.

Dorothy and I shared all the joys and sorrows of growing girls. Because I was an A student, Mrs. Zapp considered me a good friend for Dorothy and always welcomed me into their home. As for me, I thought it was a wonderful treat to be Dorothy's friend. It meant that I could eat her delicious breakfast every morning, go on family vacations to her grandmother's farm, and join her family for luscious Christmas festivities.

Some of my fondest childhood memories are of the Zapps' Christmas trees. Each tree reached to the top of their very high ceiling and seemed to fill the entire room. In those days, nobody used store-bought ornaments, and so the Zapps' trees were strung with popcorn and cranberries, and apples and oranges. Each year, it seemed that they had the most beautiful Christmas tree in the entire world!

Although I didn't realize it at the time, my friendship with Dorothy was making me more competitive. I was aware that I was supposed to be someone she looked up to, and so of course this was another reason I had to keep up the straight As. Besides, when Dorothy made an A, I had to make an A-plus. This competition extended into other areas as well. For example, if Dorothy sold twelve May Fete tickets, I had to sell twenty. Her friendship offered me so much that all I could do was try to be worthy of her. Even so, Dorothy and I willingly shared everything, and neither of us ever felt envy for the other.

About the time we graduated from Dow Junior High School, Dorothy's father received a promotion, and the family moved to a larger house on the "right" side of town. I was so impressed that I still remember the address—4024 Woodleigh. After the move there was a time when we didn't see as much of one another, but as adults we were able to reestablish the bond. It was a wonderful friendship—and is to this day!

Another lasting and influential friendship was to begin during those early years. Like Dorothy, Tillie Bass came from a family that was much more affluent than mine. Her father was a chief of detectives with the Houston police force, and I considered him to be a very important person. Tillie and her mother knew that I had to cook and keep house for my father, and so each took me under her wing. Those two ladies certainly taught me many, many things I needed to know! Tillie was a little older than I, and because of our age difference, I felt that I really had to strive to keep up. I guess I was afraid that if I didn't do well, she wouldn't be my friend. Thank heaven that thought never crossed her mind!

Tillie rescued me again when I was a young career woman supporting my family. In those days there was no such thing as the local day-care center or nursery school. A mother who worked outside her home had to rely on family and friends for safe and loving childcare. Tillie lived across the street from me, and when I went out to conduct sales presentations, she took care of my children. Our friendship grew over the years. (I used to joke that Tillie became that "wife" I needed during all those years I struggled up the ladder of success. It's a joke I never had to explain to a fellow career woman.)

By the time I reached high school, my competitive spirit was deep-rooted. I continued to make straight As, and I would have liked to be my class valedictorian. But I decided to finish high school in three rather than four years, and graduating from summer school ruined my chances. My first experience with envy came when I watched my friend Dorothy begin her study at Rice Institute. My family simply could not afford to send me to college, and in those days scholarships were rare.

So what could I do to compete with my friends who were able to further their formal educations? I knew that it had to be something great. And what seemed great to a seventeen-year-old girl in those days? You're right; I got married. He was a member of a musical group called the Hawaiian Strummers and a very big radio star in Houston. I thought he was a tremendous catch—sort of the Elvis Presley of the time. Maybe I couldn't go to college, but there was no doubt that *this* was a real feather in my cap!

It was also the first time my competitive spirit created a real problem, because it drove me to do something I would later regret. We began our family and started to build a life together. But by the time my husband's work took us to Dallas, our young marriage had become very unhappy. And when he left to serve in World War II, I became the sole emotional and financial support of our three children. The worst blow was yet to come—my husband returned from the war and announced that he wanted a divorce. It was the lowest point of my life. I had developed a sense of worth for my abilities as a wife and mother, and yet on that day I felt like a complete and total failure. Nothing had ever struck me so hard.

But I didn't have time to sit around feeling sorry for myself—I had three children to raise. To do that, I had to have a good-paying job with flexible hours. The flexibility was essential, because I knew that I wanted to spend time with my children when they needed me. Direct sales was a natural solution, and so I became a dealer for Stanley Home Products.

I enjoyed selling, but nothing excited me quite as much as company contests. It was just that old competitive spirit of mine. I particularly remember one contest that *really* fired me up. The Stanley Home Products Company announced that whoever recruited the greatest number of new dealers in a single week would be crowned "Miss Dallas." Well, I decided that was the only way I would ever be "Miss Dallas," so I was determined to win.

Our sales were usually achieved in a group presentation called a "party." As many as twenty-five people would be invited to the home of a "hostess," where the sales representative would demonstrate and sell Stanley Products. It was essential that I generate enough sales to pay my bills, so I was holding at least three Stanley parties each day. I knew that I couldn't hold all those parties *and* win a recruiting contest, so I arranged for other Stanley dealers to take my place at my scheduled presentations for a week. That way I could concentrate on recruiting new people.

I reasoned that I had one terrific source for new recruits— my date book. Because I had been conducting so many parties, it was just crammed with the names of my former hostesses. I sat down and started to work. I telephoned every hostess in my date book. Someone may have told me earlier that she was not interested in becoming a dealer, but circumstances can change. So I called *everyone!*

I would say, "Hi, Betty Ann. My company is planning to add some additional people in your area, and when I asked myself who would be just great doing what I do, I thought of *you!* Have you ever thought about going to work?"

She might answer hesitantly, "Well, Mary Kay, I just don't know."

So I would reply, "I'm going to be out your way this afternoon. I'd love to talk to you for a few minutes and bring you some literature to read. Would about two o'clock be convenient?"

All week I used the mornings to call former hostesses and make appointments. Then I spent the afternoons recruiting. I wanted to win that contest, and with seventeen recruits in a single week, I did! I was willing to give up a lot of sales commissions to win, but as it turned out, I earned almost as much money as usual. You see, many of the women I called declined my invitation to join our company, but in closing they said, "I'm glad you called; I need some—" or "My sister-in-law was just talking to me about having a party."

It doesn't look like much now, but I still have that "Miss Dallas" ribbon. Recognition was as vital to me as money. I was convinced that I wasn't the only competitive woman around, so when I set out to form my dream company, I remembered that important point. I believed that even if they wouldn't work that hard for money, there were women who would work very hard for recognition. Because I wanted a company that utilized the best elements of competition, I carefully avoided contests in which there could be only one, two, or three winners. I am convinced that competition is most productive when you are competing with yourself. So at Mary Kay Cosmetics, everyone can be a winner!

Just as my "Miss Dallas" ribbon was a symbol of my victory, every organization devises its own set of symbols. Once I worked for a company that awarded little loving cups for meeting a $1,000 monthly wholesale quota. Surely you know that I did my best to get as many as I could. I put them on the mantel until I ran out of space, and soon there were so many that they ended up in a box in the closet. The only fun I ever had with them was when people asked, "What are all those loving cups for?" I'd answer, "For loving, of course."

That taught me that symbols should be both pretty *and* useful. At Mary Kay, we gained international recognition for "symbols" such as automobiles, furs, dream vacations, and diamonds. But it all began with something I called the Golden Goblet Club. My intent was simple enough: for each monthly wholesale transaction of $1,000, a Consultant would win a beautiful, gold-plated goblet. When someone had completed a set of twelve, she would then win a matching tray. After twenty, she would win a pitcher; and soon she would have a beautiful set for her dining room.

I was so excited when I told Richard my plan. "All she has to do to win a golden goblet is to sell $1,000 worth of whole-sale merchandise in a month."

Richard looked at me in disbelief. "We're dealing with *reality*," he said. "Our top people sell approximately $150 a week. And you're talking about selling $1,000 a month? Do you think they're going to do that to win a stupid cup?"

You must realize that this was back in the days when we were still publishing the names of people who sold $100 or more in a single week—all five of them, that is. But I remembered the Miss Dallas contest. Recognition is the key, I thought.

"Yes, Richard," I said firmly, "they will work for it. This is going to be a very exclusive club. Only a few people will own a golden goblet, and they'll do it because they want the recognition the goblet symbolizes."

"I think you've lost your mind," he said. In his opinion, no one in the world would knock herself out to win a goblet— even if it was gold-plated!

But a lot of women did. They competed against their own past records in order to win those goblets. After a year or two, we had to stop inscribing them—we were just giving out too many. And then in a few more years, we began getting inquiries as to whether or not the company would consider buying them back, because many Consultants simply had no use for scores and scores of golden goblets!

From this pioneer program we developed the Ladder of Success, and it, too, is based on the principle that a person competes best when she competes against herself. The symbol for this competition is a gold pin on which each rung and each jewel represents a different personal plateau. Consultants and Sales Directors wear their Ladders of Success with great pride. And everyone knows that a person whose ladder is covered with diamonds is one of our star performers. It's like wearing a straight-A report card on your lapel.

At Mary Kay Cosmetics we try to have contests in which *everyone* has a chance at victory. I've seen too many competitions in which there was a first, second, and third prize—while everyone else lost. Once I was employed as a national training director for a direct-sales company that used such methods to "motivate" people. Because I was training the sales force, it was necessary for me to travel to many different cities. I used to say that what I needed most in that job was an asbestos suit, because everywhere I went I had to put out fires before I could get down to training. You can neither *teach* nor *motivate* people who are at one another's throats.

I knew that in my company I did not want to see anyone step on someone else to win a contest. That kind of competition is only destructive! Andrew Carnegie once said, "The first man gets the oyster, the second man gets the shell." A competition in which there's only *one* winner may motivate some people, but I believe that it usually produces adverse effects. At Mary Kay Cosmetics, everyone has an opportunity to get the oyster, the shell, *and the pearl.* But we go a step further—instead of pearls, we award sapphires, rubies, and diamonds.

Today, Mary Kay Cosmetics is more than a post-retirement idea or wishful thinking. It has become a reality—and, for me, a dream come true. The beautiful part is that every day I see the dream come true for other women.

3

My Dream Company

I SPENT TWENTY-FIVE YEARS building a career in a business world dominated by men. And I can honestly say that when I retired in 1963, thoughts of organizing my own company never entered my mind.

But I had some general opinions regarding the structure and operation of a successful business, and some specific opinions about how women might overcome the obstacles I had encountered. So I decided to write a book. My career had evolved into the area of staff development and training, so I thought of this as a guide for career women. I began by listing all the good things I had observed in my professional life and how I felt a business should be conducted in accordance with the golden rule. If an employer would treat employees and customers as he or she wished to be treated—all would profit. As my list grew, I began to dream of a company in which women had the opportunity to fully utilize their skills and talents. They could, in fact, enjoy the rewards appropriate for any goal they were smart enough to reach.

"Wouldn't it be *marvelous*," I kept thinking, "if someone would actually start such a company? I'd love to work for an organization like this." Suddenly I realized that I didn't have to just sit and wish—I could start that dream company myself! All I needed was a product that women would be comfortable selling. One night, as I was preparing for bed, the answer came to me and seemed so obvious: the skin-care products that I loved and had been using for years would be perfect for my dream company.

I had discovered these products in the early 1950s at a Stanley Home Products party. This particular party was attended by about twenty women whose ages ranged from nineteen to seventy. As I demonstrated the Stanley Products, I kept looking at the people who were gathered before me and wondering how women of such varied ages could *each* have a "perfect" complexion. It was the year those "pink lightbulbs" came on the market that promised to make every woman look as if she were "bathed in candlelight," but just lightbulbs could not explain the beautiful complexions I was observing.

After my sales presentation, we gathered in the kitchen for coffee, and it was here that I noticed my hostess handing out little white jars with black tops and penciled labels. As she distributed the items, she made notations in a composition book and gave instructions such as, "Now, let's see, you've used number three for two weeks, so use number four for seventeen days."

This was surely the secret of those beautiful complexions! Because the hostess had not offered me any of these creams, I asked, "What are you doing?" She explained that these people were her "guinea pigs," and that she felt she could take credit for the skin of everyone in that room. Everyone except me!

Then she examined my skin carefully and discovered that I had a problem with "whiteheads." In front of twenty women, she also added, "and you have aging skin!" Not a particularly flattering statement—but, of course, I knew that it was true. That night she gave me a shoe box containing the products that were the predecessors of today's Mary Kay "Basic Set." What we know as Skin Freshener was in one of her old prescription bottles, and the other products were packaged in recycled jars. A direction sheet was in the box, complete with very poor grammar and misspelled words.

I must have looked a little dubious when I saw how these items were packaged, because the women around me began telling of the remarkable improvements in their complexions. It was true that they all looked great, but in the back of my mind I thought, "This just can't be all that good; she's really got these women brainwashed."

It took me a day or two to even try the samples she had given me, but one afternoon I gave myself a facial. When my ten-year-old son Richard came home from school, he gave me a kiss on the cheek and said, "Gee, Mom, you feel smooth!" I knew that I was on to something.

Soon I was a loyal fan, eager to learn all that I could about the origin of these wonderful skin-care products. My former hostess told me that she had received the formulations from her father, a tanner of hides! He had noticed that his hands looked younger than his face, and his only explanation was that his hands were constantly in the solutions he used in his work. He decided that if these tanning solutions could turn stiff, ugly "big-pored" hides into soft leather like a glove, they must be doing the same thing for his skin. So he began to experiment by putting modified tanning solutions on his face. When he died at the age of seventy-three, his experiments had given him the skin tone and elasticity normally seen in much younger men.

He had proven his point, but no woman would ever do what he had done, because his "face tanning" process was time-consuming, smelly, and obnoxious. Everyone except his daughter ridiculed his idea. She moved to Dallas to study cosmetology and eventually modified his formulas into creams and lotions gentle enough for a woman's skin. It was these products that I had seen in her kitchen the night of my sales presentation. For several years I returned to her home, bought the odd-shaped little jars, and introduced the wonderful products to my family and friends. My own mother became an ardent consumer. One Thanksgiving, Mother was too ill to travel, so I went to Houston to visit her. During much of my visit, she felt so bad about her appearance that she didn't even want to come out of her room. I left a portion of my skin-care products and said, "I don't know if they will help, but they've done great things for my skin. Give them a try."

She did. And she began a daily program with Night Cream, Cleansing Cream, Masque, Skin Freshener, and foundation. When I visited at Christmas, my mother had also become a firm believer in the special products. She was so faithful to her skin-care regimen that when she died at the age of eighty-seven, her skin was beautiful and few people believed she was more than sixty.

I knew that the products were special, so in 1963, I bought the original formulas from the tanner's heirs. I also knew that with the right packaging, an innovative marketing concept, and a lot of hard work, my dream company could become a reality.

When starting a company the usual process is to establish monetary goals, such as "We're going to do $100,000 the first year." So it's natural that I'm often asked about my financial objectives when we first started Mary Kay Cosmetics. My answer usually surprises people—I didn't have any. My objective was to give women the opportunity to do anything they were smart enough to do. And so to me, "P & L" meant much more than profit and loss; it meant *people* and *love*.

A few years before developing the idea for Mary Kay Cosmetics, I remarried. And until his fatal heart attack, my husband handled the administrative end of our business plan, while I was in charge of marketing. Often he would explain to me how we had to buy our goods at one price and sell them for X amount more to the consumer. "That's how a business keeps from going broke, Mary Kay," he'd say. His advice just went in one ear and out the other. I wasn't interested in the dollars-and-cents part of any business; my interest in 1963 was in offering women opportunities that didn't exist any-where else. At that time, the vast majority of companies sim-ply didn't make room in their executive suites for women. Oh yes, if a woman was really exceptional, she might become an assistant to a senior officer. But that was about as far as she could go. In twenty-five years I had seen countless capable individuals held back only because they were female.

I myself had been frustrated by the lack of opportunity for women. One company paid me $25,000 a year to be its national training director, but, in truth, I was acting as the national *sales manager*—and for a salary much less than the job was worth. Then there were the times when I would be asked to take a man out on the road to train him, and after six months of training, he would be brought back to Dallas, made my superior, and given twice my salary! It happened more than once. What really angered me was when I was told that these men earned more because they had families to sup-port. I had a family to support, too. In those days, it seemed that a woman's brains were worth only fifty cents on the dol-lar in a male-run corporation. Even *more insulting* was the way a woman's ideas were rarely respected. I became enraged every time I presented a good marketing plan and was dismissed with, "Mary Kay, you're thinking just like a woman." I knew that in *my* company "thinking like a woman" was going to be an asset, not a liability!

But that wasn't all; I had some other unique plans for my dream company. After working for several direct-sales organi-zations, I knew that I wanted to eliminate assigned territories. I remembered when I was earning $1,000 a month in commis-sions from my unit sales and my husband took a new job in St. Louis. Because I couldn't take my unit with me, I lost all the commissions on the people I had recruited, trained, and motivated for eight years. I thought this was patently unfair. I had built the territory, but someone else inherited those ter-rific salespeople *and* the commissions on their sales.

At Mary Kay Cosmetics, we don't have territories. A Beauty Consultant can be on vacation in Hawaii or California or anywhere else and recruit a new Consultant. She can live in Cleveland and be visiting her sister in Omaha when she recruits someone. In any case, as the recruiter she can receive a personal recruit commission on the wholesale purchases of her recruit. To carry the example further, the Director in Omaha will take that new recruit under her wing, train her, include her in the Omaha unit meetings, and guide her right up the Ladder of Success. And yet all eligible commissions will go back to Cleveland and the woman who originally brought that new person into the company. We call this our "adoptee" program.

The Omaha recruit may go on to recruit additional people, and as long as both she and her Cleveland sponsor stay active within the company, the recruiter can receive commissions on the recruit's sales activity.

Ask any financial adviser, and he or she will tell you that this system cannot possibly work. But it does work. Today Mary Kay Cosmetics has thousands of Sales Directors, and most of them work in more than one state. Many work in a dozen or more. Each Sales Director reaps the benefits from her recruits in other cities and helps local recruits in return.

The critics say, "Why should anybody work to develop an adoptee—and never get a cent of commission? Why should *I* work to bring *your* person up the Ladder of Success so that *you* can get all the commissions? You're crazy!" But our Sales Directors don't think that way. Some of them have seventy-five to one hundred adoptees, and it can indeed represent a substantial drain on an individual's time and energy. But each Sales Director thinks, "I'm helping her, but someone else is helping *my* recruits in other cities." The system works. And while I agree that such a program could be difficult to implement into an existing company, I believe it would work for any beginning organization.

This system works because it is based upon the golden rule, or as we sometimes refer to it, the "Go-Give" principle. At Mary Kay Cosmetics, we focus on *giving*, not just *getting*, and we use this philosophy in every aspect of the company. For example, we use the Go-Give principle when teaching our Beauty Consultants the art of customer relations. We constantly stress that a Consultant must never have dollar signs in her eyes or think, "How much can I sell these people today?" Instead, she must think in terms of "What can I do today so that these women will leave here feeling better about themselves? How can I help each woman develop a more positive self-image?" We know that if a woman feels pretty on the outside, she becomes prettier on the inside, too. In addition, she goes on to become a better member of her family and of her community.

Another cornerstone of Mary Kay Cosmetics was my desire to give consumers the opportunity to learn about cosmetics in a natural, relaxed environment *before* they buy a single item. I had learned long before starting the company that most women understand neither *why* they are buying a specific product nor *how* that product will meet their individual skin-care needs. In short, they don't know how to take care of their skin. The normal pattern is to buy a jar of this from a department store, buy a jar of that from a drugstore, add something else from someplace else, and then use it all together in a haphazard fashion. I knew this was true because I had done it myself. I had bought hundreds of dollars' worth of cosmetics that I never used. They all looked terrific in the store, but when I got home, they never seemed to do what I expected. I saw this situation as a wonderful opportunity to teach women about total skin care.

To accomplish this, I created the small sales presentation (or skin-care class) for no more than five or six women. While other direct-sales companies stressed "parties" and asked a hostess to provide twelve to twenty-five people for the product demonstration, I realized that such a system created numerous problems. First, many hostesses felt that their homes would not hold a crowd of this size. Others would say, "I must serve refreshments, and I don't have that many good cups!" But most of all, everyone recognized that such large demonstrations were impersonal. I wanted our Consultants to work with small groups so that each person would receive personal attention. When instructing just five or six people, our Consultant can evaluate the needs of each woman and answer every question. She can, for example, teach a woman how to cleanse her skin, how to make her thin lips look fuller, or how to use contouring techniques to make her round face appear more oval. Personalizing the beauty process became our specialty. I wanted every woman to leave a Mary Kay skin-care class knowing how to properly maintain healthy skin, as well as the best ways to use cosmetics to enhance her own natural beauty.

As the popularity of our methods grew, we were approached about selling Mary Kay products in department stores. But that was not the answer for us. Most women are too self-conscious to remove their cosmetics in a public place or to take shopping time for a lengthy consultation. And without proper instruction, a woman could look like Linda Evans in the store and Dracula when she tried to re-create "the look" at home. In a home environment, each woman can learn to apply her own makeup in front of her own mirror and in natural light. Once this instructional process is complete, she can correctly apply what she has learned today, tomorrow, and forever.

Equally important is the fact that when a woman has an opportunity to learn about skin care in this way, she will buy only those products that meet her individual needs. As I've indicated, our policy at Mary Kay skin-care classes is to instruct—not sell. In fact, we attract many Beauty Consultants who wouldn't be with us if they had to high-pressure a customer. But all these women do share two personality characteristics: they like helping people and they like *presenting* new ideas and important information. Every successful Consultant enjoys presenting our products in an enthusiastic and knowledgeable manner. In short, everyone loves being a skin-care teacher. In keeping with our educational philosophy, we are one of the few companies to offer an unconditional money-back guarantee. After all, if you try a product and learn that it is inappropriate for you, that too is progress. For when you do make the correct choice, you will become just the kind of consumer we like to see.

Another problem I intended to avoid in my dream company was the difficulties encountered when the customer receives her merchandise two or three weeks after purchase. Personally, I'm too impetuous for that! When I want something, I want it right now; I don't like waiting three weeks. After all, in three weeks I may forget why I wanted it in the first place. These distribution problems are always magnified when a direct-sales company tries to maintain a product line of several hundred items. No independent Beauty Consultant can have such an inventory available for immediate delivery. So at Mary Kay Cosmetics, our philosophy is to purposely limit ourselves to a minimum number of essential skin-care and glamour items. We encourage each Consultant to take an order, deliver the product, and collect her money the day of the sales presentation. We don't require our Consultants to purchase any specific quantity, but those who do maintain an adequate inventory quickly learn that people will buy more readily when they can take their products home with them.

I told you at the beginning of this chapter that I wanted to give women the opportunity to reach their full potential. Marketing strategies, revolutionary commission procedures, product development, and distribution techniques were all essential elements of my plan—but I realized that none of my dreams would last if we couldn't establish a sound fiscal policy. And yes, that does mean money—I had to face dollars and cents. My problem was how to maintain our company's solvency and still provide our Consultants with the best possible commission scale. My answer was to deal in cash. Bad debts are the primary reason for failure in other direct-sales companies. Many excellent sales representatives are lost, not because they are dishonest but because they are poor money managers.

At Mary Kay Cosmetics, our Consultants and Directors pay in advance for every item of merchandise, and they pay with a cashier's check, money order, Mastercard or Visa. We accept no personal checks for product orders. This is not a lack of trust; it is simply our absolute belief in the wisdom expressed in our American system of cash-and-carry capitalism. No Mary Kay Consultant can run up a debt with our company, and as a result, we have very few accounts receivable and no expense of collecting bad debts. Best of all, everyone benefits because we pass our savings on in the form of higher commissions. Every Mary Kay Consultant is an independent businessperson, and we encourage each and every one to conduct her own business in this same fashion.

Most financial experts marvel at our system—it's unheard of in a company of our size. In fact, when I began the company, my accountant looked at my plans for inventory distribution and my high commission schedule and said, "There's no way, Mary Kay. You can't demand cash and then pay this many cents out of every dollar you make. You can't operate like that; it just won't work." But my son and new business partner had worked out every detail. Richard said it would work, and I knew that it *would!*

My accountant was not the only disbeliever. Many well-intentioned people, including my attorney, assured me that my company would fail. After all, who ever *heard* of a company based on the golden rule? My attorney even went so far as to send to Washington, D.C., for a pamphlet detailing how many cosmetics companies were going broke each year. Over and over people said to me, "Mary Kay, you're *dreaming.*"

Yes, I was dreaming; that's how it all started. But when I look back at what has happened in this company, I am convinced that it was more than the dream of one woman. I believe that long before I sat down to write my training guide and develop my dream, God in His infinite wisdom had a plan. His plan was to use my dream company as a vehicle for women all over the world. And instead of a tightly closed corporate door bearing the sign "For Men Only," our company has an open portal that bears the invitation "Everyone Welcome—*Especially* Women."

4

Mary Kay Cosmetics— The Early Years

IT'S BECOME TRADITIONAL for our entire family to gather at my house on Thanksgiving Day. A few years ago I was preparing for the holiday crowd (there were going to be fifty-three of us!), when I realized that the two huge turkeys I had bought wouldn't fit in my oven at the same time. This was going to be a real problem, for while I could have cooked one turkey the day before Thanksgiving, I thought that it might lose some of that good "fresh-baked" flavor. And while I had a microwave, I liked my turkey cooked long and slow.

Then I remembered something stored in my garage: my trusty old turkey roaster. I dusted it off and tested it, and sure enough, it still worked. "Good ol' faithful," I thought, "you never let me down." Suddenly my mind was flooded with many good memories. I had used that turkey roaster back in 1964 when I cooked for our company's first-anniversary Seminar.

As I cleaned it up, I felt like pinching myself to see if I was dreaming. It seemed like a lifetime ago, but it was just a couple of decades. "We've come a long way, baby!" I told that old roaster.

The first headquarters for Mary Kay Cosmetics was a five-hundred-square-foot storefront in Exchange Park, a large bank and office building complex in Dallas. As I have said, we opened the doors on Friday, September 13, 1963—exactly one month to the day after my husband died. I had invested what I thought was a fortune ($5,000) in formulations, jars, and used office equipment, and was starting out on what was to become quite an adventure.

Richard and I had great hopes for our location; the Exchange Bank occupied a major portion of the building's first floor, and a number of national companies occupied most of the remaining floors. There were also several small businesses, including a coffee shop, a drugstore, and a restaurant. Our offices were on a mall, which catered to the five thousand women who worked throughout the building complex. We were certain that we would get lots of sales from that captive market; they'd go right past us each morning on the way to work, and then they'd go right past us again every evening. For a long time after our opening, we were absolutely correct—they went right past! In the morning they were rushing to get to work on time, and in the evening they were anxious to get home. Our only advantage was that they did get coffee breaks twice a day. Before long we learned to give the fastest facials you've ever seen. We even learned how to dry the masque quickly with an electric fan.

But as I stated, we were still full of hope. And truthfully, we had anticipated that it would be difficult getting women to stop in to learn about an unknown line of cosmetics. Women will often say, "I've been using Brand X for years and I'm perfectly satisfied." We needed something to attract customers, and I thought of offering custom wigs. In 1963, wigs were a very hot item, so I went to Florida for a training course and we bought an inventory of high-quality human-hair wigs. We were ready for business. If we didn't succeed, I knew I'd be back working for someone for the rest of my life.

It was Richard's idea to have a glamorous grand opening. We hired a very famous wig stylist, Renée of Paris, to style all wigs purchased that day, and we hired a darling little model to serve champagne to the customers. I will admit that I was never comfortable with champagne and a model, but I accepted the judgment that I was being old-fashioned and went along with it. And sure enough, who do you think the model attracted? The men in the building—not the women. Nevertheless, we sold about a dozen wigs to those women who did come in, and Renée styled them all very elegantly. Naturally the women who were blond bought brunette wigs, and the brunettes all wanted blond wigs.

We were very excited about those first-day sales until Monday morning. That's when we learned that it's a terrible mistake to buy a wig that's noticeably different from your own hair. A wig should supplement a woman's wardrobe, and help her look good when she doesn't have time to style her hair. But we didn't realize how important it was to stress this fact to our customers, and so we sold them anything they wanted. Of course as soon as they went home family and friends cried something like, "Goldilocks! What in the world happened to you?" We did not have a return policy for custom-styled wigs, but we honored every request until each customer was satisfied.

After that experience, we were very careful to advise women as to the color of wigs they should select. And actually, the wigs did prove to be a drawing card, many times attracting women who also bought cosmetics. Our Beauty Consultants took the wigs to skin care classes, but because our primary concern was skin care, they weren't brought out until the facials were completed. Taking wigs to classes presented all kinds of new problems. First, a wig styled for one person can look totally incorrect on someone else. Therefore, the Consultants had to take several of those expensive wigs everywhere they went. And if a wig was not handled carefully, the set could easily be ruined.

Finally, the wigs took up a lot of space in our Exchange Park storefront. We styled and stored them in the back, so that room was always cluttered with hair dryers and curlers. Because we were seeing customers in the front room, we kept it nicely decorated, but the "wig paraphernalia" meant that we had no place to store our cosmetics. Finally we were forced to rent a basement storage area. Our problems had just begun, because in order to get to the inventory, you had to go out in the mall, walk half a block, go down a long flight of stairs, and then walk another hundred yards once you got to the basement. It amounted to a two-block hike. Richard was handling our bookkeeping, but he also had the assignment of going down to storage to fill orders.

I always insisted that Richard dress like a businessman (even though he still looked like a teenager). Once a sale was made, he would formally take the order saying, "Yes, ma'am, I'll be right back." Then he would head off for the stairs, peeling off his coat as he ran through the mall. By the time he reached the storage area, he'd have his coat and tie off. Once the order was assembled, he'd put his coat and tie on, straighten his shoulders, run back to the showroom, and hand the customer the order, just as dignified as you please. But there was no doubt that he was running himself to death, up and down those steps. And as our business grew, his administrative duties grew as well. He was finally saved when his older brother, Ben, joined our business. Ben worked out of the basement storage area, and we simply called the orders in to him.

In early 1965, Richard declared, "I've had it with these wigs. We've got to get rid of them!" It *was* getting ridiculous. We estimated that it was taking eight hours of a Consultant's time to sell one wig. First she had to bring the customer in to sell and fit the wig, then she had to bring the customer back a second time to pick up the finished product. It was time-consuming for everyone. Taking the wigs out of our line turned out to be an excellent decision. Our Consultants zeroed in on the skin-care products, and our sales climbed $20,000 the very next month.

By now we were truly a family company, and soon we were joined by my daughter, Marylyn. When our business was just two months old, I had visited Marylyn at her home in Houston and given her a beauty case full of our products. No training manual, mind you—just a beauty case. "Do something with this," I had said. Of course, Marylyn had been using the products for years, so there was no need to talk her into anything. In addition to caring for her children, Marylyn became one of our first Directors. And for four years (until medical problems with her back forced her to leave the business) she was one of our best representatives. I'm sure that if she had been able to continue, she would have become a top Director in our organization.

My first Beauty Consultants—all nine of them—came with us because they were friends, and because they trusted us when we said we would make it. There were other (maybe even more experienced) salespeople I would have longed to recruit, but I had made a firm decision not to proselytize people working with other direct-sales companies. My very first Consultant, Dalene White, had previously worked for my husband's company, and she came with me as her way of being a good friend. Today, Dalene is one of our National Sales Directors, and her earnings have exceeded any of her wildest dreams. She was to become one of our very first Mary Kay Millionaires. That's an honor bestowed when a National Sales Director earns more than $1 million in commissions. To date, we have had seventy-four Mary Kay Millionaires, twenty-seven of whom have become multimillionaires. Not bad for an operation that started out with "a hope and a prayer."

Some of those original Consultants had intended to join us on just a temporary basis. Apparently, I was so enthusiastic, they couldn't say no. There were other people, of course, who did say no, and they just watched and waited for us to go broke. With hindsight, you might say that they made a mistake, but remember, back then it really looked as if we didn't know what we were doing. Everything was still experimen-tal—we just kept "plugging along" doing things by the Golden Rule.

It is important for managers to have "field experience" if they are to be of real value to their sales force. So in the begin-ning I also gave sales presentations. But I learned that people really don't appreciate having the owner of the company make initial contact. "You *own* this company and you're at my house giving facials?" they would ask. "Must be an awfully small company." Apparently they presumed that if the com-pany was that small, the products couldn't be very good. I dearly loved giving skin-care classes, but before long I was forced to admit, from my own past experiences and from what the Consultants were telling me, that it would be better if I didn't. But over a period of time, we were able to develop a uniform sales presentation and a sales training program.

One of the things I concentrated on during our first years was the development of a Consultant instruction manual. I worked very, very hard on it, and when I got the first one ready, I thought it was rather impressive. It had five pages! And one of them was a "Welcome Letter"! Today the Mary Kay Consultants Guide has more than two hundred pages. It has evolved as our successful Directors learned and shared their knowledge.

We began with a Basic Skin Care Set consisting of Cleans-ing Cream, Magic Masque, Skin Freshener, Night Cream, and Day Radiance Foundation. The products were in little jars and bottles, and each Consultant had a set that she would pass around for every woman to use. That was before we really knew about sanitation and how easily microorganisms from one person's skin can be harmful to someone else. As I think about it now, I'm aghast that we didn't know any better!

We always knew that the five items in the Basic Set worked together to help maintain a woman's skin and keep it beautiful. But in the beginning, we would break the set and sell a woman any individual item she requested. A few months later we sometimes got calls from women who had bought only a few items, and they would say, "It didn't work for me. What happened?" In the beginning, we even divided a foundation if that's what the customer wanted. This product came in a variety of skin tones and in a yellow color base for covering red spots or blotches. If a Consultant was working with three different people, each of whom only wanted a small amount of something, such as yellow Day Radiance foundation, the Consultant would take a knife and some wax paper, divide one Day Radiance foundation into three parts and let the customers draw to see who got the box! I can't *believe* we did that, but we did. Breaking up the Basic Set in this manner was like giving you my recipe for chocolate cake and leaving out the chocolate or the sugar. It just isn't going to be *my* cake! For example, if you applied the masque by itself, without first cleansing the face and then following with the Skin Freshener, it could have a drying effect. The products in the Basic Set have always complemented one another. We finally concluded that we would not break the Basic Set. We decided we would rather face a consumer's initial ire than have her fail to get the desired results.

Our first inventory included the Basic Set and additional glamour items: rouge, lip and eye palettes, mascara, and eyebrow pencil. I remember that on our first day of business we stored our *entire* Mary Kay inventory on a $9.95 steel shelving unit I had purchased at Sears. Today we have approximately one hundred products in our full line (excluding shade variations), and the average Consultant probably has more inventory than the entire company had that opening day!

When we started Mary Kay Cosmetics, we thought our products were wonderful; even so, we knew that we could make them better. We now invest millions of dollars in research so that we can continue to improve and refine every product in the line. Today, there are formulas for virtually every skin type, because, as I said, personalizing the beauty process is our specialty. We want women to get the best possible results, and so we teach them how to use our products to the very best advantage.

Initially, our products were made by a private manufacturing company in Dallas. I chose this firm because it was run by a man with an excellent reputation in the cosmetics field, and we wanted someone who was both ethical and reliable. I took the formulations to the president of that company, and he calmly turned the whole thing over to his son. After our tiny order, I'm sure he thought he'd never see *us* again. But we did come back with a second order, and a third, and so on, and so on. A few years later we were in a position to invite his son to join us and head our own manufacturing division.

When we first started the business, Richard, Ben, and I put in sixteen- and eighteen-hour workdays as we struggled to do anything that had to be done. Sometimes after filling and packing orders, we would write and mimeograph our newsletter until two o'clock in the morning. But our hard work paid off. During our first three and a half months in business, we had made a small profit on $34,000 in sales. The first calendar year brought us $198,000 in wholesale sales, and at the end of the second year, we had reached the unbelievable total of $800,000!

After just one year in business, we had expanded to such a scale that we needed new offices. We moved our headquarters to 1220 Majesty Drive. Now we had three "real" offices (one each for Richard, Ben, and me), a training room, and a huge warehouse—five thousand square feet in all! It seemed like the Grand Canyon to us! And best of all—nobody had to run out into the mall and down the basement stairs.

On September 13, 1964, we held our first company convention—and we called it "Seminar." Seminar is still a big event for us (and later I will describe how it has grown to its present spectacular form). For this first one, we couldn't afford to rent space in a hotel, so we convened in the ware-house of our Majesty Drive location. I still remember how enthusiastic we all were—and how hard we tried to econo-mize! We decorated the warehouse with crêpe paper and bal-loons, and whipped up a menu of chicken, jalapeño dressing, and a Jell-O salad. We had bought little paper plates that were much too flimsy to cut on, so I cooked and boned chicken for two hundred people the week before, made the dressing, and froze everything. On the appointed day, I thawed out every-thing and reheated it in that old turkey roaster of mine. I also made a huge orange Jell-O salad filled with all kinds of good-ies. But I failed to consider that it was September, and Texas isn't all that cool in September. That Jell-O melted all over the place! But people sat, held their droopy plates on their laps, and did the best they could. Richard hired a three-piece band to entertain us, and Ellen Notley, a Director from Tyler, Texas, baked a big cake decorated with the words "Happy First Anniversary." It had been an extremely happy anniversary—at the end of our first year, the Mary Kay business family included two hundred wonderful people!

After dinner, I acted as master of ceremonies, and we had our first annual awards night. It was very modest compared with what we do now, but we were all thrilled. I keep a copy of every speech I ever give, as I often revise and update them for subsequent presentations. (No sense in wasting a good thought!) Recently, I reviewed the speeches given at past Sem-inars. Parts of a favorite speech had reappeared on several occasions, but in its original form the copy had read, "And next year, we expect to have three thousand people in our sales force!" I remember basing that statement on Richard's market projections; yet as I spoke those numbers, I really couldn't imagine it would ever come true. The following year I used the same page in my speech; only the estimate had been scratched out and replaced with the number *eleven thou-sand.* Further along in my collection, I found the identical page with the notation "Make that forty thousand!" Today, hundreds of thousands of Beauty Consultants teach women the Mary Kay system of skin care, and we're still growing. Looks as if I'll have to leave this particular spot vacant the next time my speech is reprinted—then I can just pencil in our current total.

Our growth has brought many changes. For one thing you can't feed thousands of Consultants by using a turkey roaster. The old roaster has been retired from Seminar duty, but I want you to know that it still cooks a terrific Thanksgiving dinner!

5

That Mary Kay Enthusiasm

FOR SOME REASON, singing seems to unite people. Remember when you sang those "Rah rah rah for our team" songs in high school and in college? That group spirit we all experienced is known as esprit de corps.

When I worked for Stanley Home Products, the company had a number of songs that were always sung before and during our sales meetings, and it really helped to build esprit de corps. After leaving Stanley, I joined World Gift, a company which lacked that spirit. In fact, when I first joined the company, everyone seemed a bit cold. In an attempt to break the ice, I introduced a song contest, and the people came up with dozens of World Gift songs. I watched those songs change the temperament of the entire sales force.

So when we started Mary Kay Cosmetics, I decided that we had to have a Mary Kay song contest. We would select what we thought were the best songs, sing them at Seminar, and award prizes for those that generated the most enthusiasm.

Now the secret of a well-received song is to write your own words to a popular tune. And the song most accepted within our organization evolved when someone wrote "I've Got That Mary Kay Enthusiasm" to a much-loved hymn. We sang it at every significant gathering of Mary Kay Consultants. With no irreverence intended, "That Mary Kay Enthusiasm" became something of a theme song.

Traditionally, our sales meetings are held on Mondays, and enthusiasm plays an important role in these gatherings. To many people, Monday signals the end of a carefree weekend and the beginning of a work week. But if the last week was not good for *you*, it *was* good for someone else! So we often tell our Consultants, "If you had a bad week, you need the unit meeting; if you had a good week, the unit meeting needs *you!*" When a Consultant leaves the inspiration, motivation, and enthusiasm of a Monday unit meeting, she has an entire week to let all that excitement work for her. The whole week starts off in high gear.

I believe that just as Monday meetings generate enthusiasm, a parent can generate enthusiasm in his or her family. For example, if a mother starts the day in a grumpy mood, the chances are that the whole family will leave the house with this same attitude. Even though she might not feel like it, every mother should make the effort to smile and say a cheery "Good morning; how are you?" Before long, even if she didn't feel cheerful to begin with, she'll feel better, too. Enthusiasm is contagious—even for yourself. I truly believe that if you act enthusiastic, you will become enthusiastic! Not just for a day—but for a lifetime!

One of the best examples of *making* yourself enthusiastic occurred several years ago when we asked a prominent person to address a large group of Mary Kay Directors and Consultants. His flight was delayed, so it was necessary to keep improvising the program until he arrived. Finally, I was given the signal that he had just rushed in and was waiting backstage.

Because I was the emcee, I had a page of typewritten accolades for him, and I enthusiastically began giving his introduction. While I was doing this, I could see him backstage—beating his chest and jumping up and down. For all the world, he looked just like a gorilla! I thought, "My goodness, here I am saying all these wonderful things about this man, and he has just 'flipped'!" I had never seen *anyone* act so strangely.

When I finished the introduction, he rushed on stage and gave a fantastic speech. It was truly motivating. Later, while sitting next to him at lunch, I said, "You almost scared me to death. What in the world were you *doing* back there, jumping up and down, beating on your chest like that?"

"Well, Mary Kay," he said, "my job is motivation. But some days I just don't feel like it, and this was one of those days. I've had an incredibly hectic time with my flight being delayed this morning. But I knew that you were expecting me to be an enthusiastic, vibrant, exciting speaker. I just couldn't rain on your parade, especially when I saw all those excited people in the audience. So I had to turn myself on. And I've found that if I just churn up my blood with some exercise and chest beating, I feel much better."

He became enthusiastic by using an external technique, but it's interesting to note that the word *enthusiasm* comes from a Greek word meaning "God within." And some people do seem to pull this characteristic from somewhere within themselves. You could even call it a natural talent. I'm certain that my own God-given enthusiasm was my number-one asset when I first began my sales career.

When I first learned what the gift of enthusiasm could accomplish, I was a very young homemaker; a life in sales had never entered my mind. A saleswoman named Ida Blake came to my door selling the *Child Psychology Bookshelf*, a series of instructional stories for children. Each story contained a real-life problem, a solution, and an underlying moral for the child to use in similar situations. As a young mother trying to teach her children the difference between right and wrong, I thought those were the best books I had ever seen. Unfortunately, I couldn't afford them. Sensing my interest, Ida let me keep the books over the weekend. I read every page. And when she came by to pick them up, I was heartbroken that they could not be available to my children. I told her that I was going to save my money and one day a set would belong to my family.

When she saw how excited I was, she said, "I'll tell you what, Mary Kay, if you sell ten sets of books for me, I'll give you a set for yourself." Well, that was just wonderful! I started calling my friends and the parents of my students at Tabernacle Baptist Church Sunday School. I didn't have books to show them—all I had was my enthusiasm.

Because of the way I told people these were the best books I'd ever seen, I sold ten sets in just a day and a half. I was so excited that they got excited, too. When Ida came back, she couldn't believe it! I had customers lined up so that all she had to do was go to their homes and take the orders. Later she asked, "These books are difficult to sell; how did you *do* it?"

I didn't *know* what I had done, but Ida gave me my set of books and that was all that I wanted.

Ida had other ideas. She said, "I want you to work for me—do you have a car?"

I answered, "Yes, we do, but I don't know how to drive."

We did have a ramshackle old car that my husband drove every morning to his job at the service station and every night to his musical engagements. But Ida told me to be sure he left the car for me the next day. She was going to teach me how to sell books.

She drove us out to a suburb, and we knocked on doors all day long. By the end of that day, I was exhausted. I had never been so tired in my life. We didn't make a single sale. In fact, not one person was even remotely interested. I had sold ten sets in a day and a half, and I couldn't understand why she was having so much trouble. I hadn't realized the power of my enthusiasm.

At five o'clock that evening, Ida got in on the passenger's side of the car and announced, "You're driving home."

"But I don't know how to drive."

That didn't matter to Ida. She had decided that if I was going to be a saleswoman, I had to know how to drive. "You're going to learn right now," she said. She gave me one quick lesson, and off we went—right into the Houston rush hour, with its bumper-to-bumper traffic. I practically stripped the gears, but we did get home. The next day, I guess I let my enthusiasm for my new skill as a driver get the best of me. I drove down to my mother's restaurant—very proud of myself—and knocked down two of the three posts holding the porch above the sidewalk. The posts fell right on top of the car and just about finished it.

Nevertheless, I was learning how to drive, and thanks to Ida Blake I had my first sales job. During the next nine months, I sold $25,000 worth of books. And at a 30 to 40 percent commission, I was making good money. But I was still to learn an important lesson about customer relations. When I saw my friends, they were often angry with me because of their purchases. It wasn't a flaw in the product; they all agreed that the books were very good. But they weren't being used. My customers seemed to blame me because my enthusiasm had led them to buy books they did not fully utilize. Well, what good are books that aren't read? Their laziness was certainly not my fault. Still, I learned that the customer must be *taught* how to successfully use the product; and it was a principle I was to employ later when starting Mary Kay Cosmetics.

My next job brought me additional sales experience. My husband had lost his job at the service station, so as a team we went to work selling cookware. Our specialty items were high-quality, alloy pressure cookers and double frying pans. Sales were initiated by actual cooking demonstrations, and that's where I came in. I would purchase the food and prepare it during the day, and on the evening of the demonstration, we would bring everything into the prospect's home and put on a dinner party. The menu was always the same: green beans, ham, sweet potatoes, and a cake; preparing it was supposed to look like child's play. But I had spent a great deal of time purchasing the finest cut of ham, selecting the most tender green beans and sweet potatoes, carefully preparing them, and premixing the cake batter. My husband would give the sales presentation to several couples in the living room, and I would be back in the kitchen cooking the meal with that pressure cooker and double frying pan.

In reality, it was I who made the sales, because the wives would invariably come out into the kitchen and ask me questions like "Is it really as easy as it looks?" And because the cookware truly was wonderful, I would answer, "Yes!"

Each dinner was fabulous, but it was food we couldn't afford to buy for ourselves. If there was any food left over after the demonstration, it became our dinner. If our prospective customers ate it all, we just didn't eat that night.

Eventually we were forced to quit. It was during the Depression, and most people simply couldn't afford new cookware. Besides, selling it took what I considered a hard sell, and I was never very good at that.

At Mary Kay Cosmetics, we discourage aggressive selling. We prefer to *teach* skin care, and simply express our enthusiasm for our product. We look for Consultants who share our educational philosophy, not those who want to use a hard sell. As a result, our sales force includes hundreds of former teachers and nurses. When they discover that they can earn as much as, or even *more* than they did in former positions, being a Mary Kay Beauty Consultant becomes an exciting and rewarding career.

I think most consumers appreciate the low-key presentation style we sometimes call "polite persuasion." We present our skin-care line in an enthusiastic, knowledgeable manner, and most of us feel it simply sells itself. Frequently we receive letters from customers and hostesses complimenting our Consultants for their polite and professional presentations.

"My loving mother"

Baby Mary Kay

At the age of seven

High-school graduation

As a young saleswoman

Mary Kay with her sons, Ben and Richard, and office staff in front of the company's corporate building in 1964

Mary Kay signs her autobiography during a nationwide book tour.

Mary Kay in 1973

With husband Mel Ash, 1979

Mary Kay with her family: as of 1994, May Kay has sixteen grandchildren and twenty-four great-grandchildren.

This kind of selling also ensures customer loyalty and enthusiasm for our products. Because we aren't aggressive, customers trust us in a way they wouldn't trust a company that used pressure techniques.

It's also common for a customer's spouse to be enthusiastic about our products. One time the receptionist buzzed me and said, "Mary Kay, there's a man on the line who is asking to speak to the real thing—if there is one."

"What does he want?" I asked.

"He won't say; he just said he'll only talk to the real thing."

I told her to put him on, and I *never* heard a man talk so fast. I think he was afraid the real thing would hang up! He said, "Mary Kay, I called to thank you for saving my marriage."

Because I didn't know this man, I couldn't imagine how I might have saved his marriage. But before I could ask, he continued, "My wife and I have been married for eight years, and when we first met, she looked like something right out of the pages of *Vogue* magazine. She had every hair in place, a beautiful face, and a fabulous figure. Then she became pregnant and was sick for the entire nine months. She lost all interest in her appearance. We had a second child, and the cycle repeated."

He was talking so quickly that I didn't have a chance to say a word.

"It got to the point," he continued, "that when I left in the morning, she would be standing there with one kid hanging onto her dirty housecoat, and another kid screaming in her arms. She never combed her hair, and she never made up her face. When I'd come home at night, the only thing that would have changed was that it was worse!

"About two months ago, she went to a Mary Kay skin-care class and bought $28 worth of that stuff." (I could tell that this amount sounded like the national debt to him.)

"But," he said, "the woman who sold it to her really did a good job! My wife probably thought that I'd be mad at her for spending $28 on cosmetics, so when she got home, she fixed her face. As soon as she saw the improvement, she had to do her hair and get dressed. When I got home that night, she looked *terrific!* It had been so long since I had seen her looking that way that I had forgotten how beautiful she really was. And the best part is that she now fixes her face and hair and gets dressed *every* morning. Besides that, she's lost twelve pounds; and I've got my old girl back. I've fallen in love with her all over again, and it's all because of you!"

Then he hung up. Those were his last words: "It's all because of you." I never got a chance to ask him who he was, or which Beauty Consultant had done such a great job. But I went immediately into a unit meeting and told them what had happened. Then I said, "How do you know that it wasn't *you* who performed this little miracle?" I still tell that story, because while few men would actually take the time to telephone, the same miracle has probably been repeated thousands of times.

Often my own enthusiasm for Mary Kay products makes a sale when I least expect it. One interesting incident occurred in 1966, when my late husband Mel and I enjoyed a delayed honeymoon trip to Rome. We were sitting in an open-air restaurant near the Colosseum—one of those places where everyone sits side by side at long tables. Mel had just finished saying, "I haven't seen *any* of those beautiful women Europe is famous for. Where *are* they?"

Just then, a gorgeous woman walked in—tall, thin, and stately. She had beautiful black hair and an ivory complexion, and she was very well dressed. We both decided she must be an Italian countess. As luck would have it, the waiter seated her next to Mel, and her husband next to me. A few minutes later, Mel took out a pack of cigarettes, and the man asked if he might have one. He explained that they had been in Europe for six weeks and that he hadn't been able to get any American cigarettes. Mel graciously gave him the pack, and the man said, "Thank you. I will treasure these."

They began talking, and the man asked Mel what business he was in. Mel told him, "I'm in a gift business, and my wife is in the cosmetics business."

The woman immediately became very interested. "Cosmetics?" she asked. "What kind?"

"Mary Kay Cosmetics," I answered. "You have probably never heard of us. We're a small company in Texas—just a little more than two years old." Then, before I knew it, I was enthusiastically telling her about our products. The purse I was carrying that evening was so small that it wouldn't even hold a lip and eye palette, so I had *nothing* to show her. But by the time we had finished dinner, she was writing a check for one of *everything* in our line! She explained that she would be back home in Acapulco in three months and asked if I would have the items sent to her by then. My enthusiasm about our products had excited her so much that she wanted to try them, *sight unseen!*

After receiving the products, she became even more excited. She kept sending in orders for three to six complete collections *every month or so.* I was amazed, because the import duty in Mexico was almost 100 percent, so a collection was costing twice the United States price. Unable to contain my curiosity, I wrote and asked what in the world she was doing with all of the cosmetics she was ordering. She explained that because she looked so radiant, her friends constantly asked what she was using. Her response was to give them facials and present the products as gifts.

Enthusiasm does spread like that. We have an expression at Mary Kay, "The speed of the leader is the speed of the gang." Just as a Consultant or a satisfied customer can generate enthusiasm in someone, a single person can also generate enthusiasm in an entire group. The best way to do this is by example. If a Director is enthusiastic, the Consultants in her unit will be enthusiastic. And I believe that our Directors set a wonderful example for their Consultants to follow. It is my feeling that each of them is "Mary Kay" to her people, and they are, in turn, "Mary Kay" to the customers.

I am thankful that I have been blessed with natural enthusiasm, because I'm certain this quality is responsible for my high energy level. Even after all these years in business, no matter how exhausted I may be the night before, I awaken each morning with renewed enthusiasm. I love what I do, and each day presents new opportunities to love and encourage each working woman to success.

I like what Ralph Waldo Emerson said, "Nothing great was ever achieved without enthusiasm." Just think, he didn't even *know* about *Mary Kay* enthusiasm!

6

Put On a Happy Face

I HAD A VERY HARD TIME accepting the divorce from my first husband. For almost a year, I felt that I had failed as a woman, as a wife, and as a person. Being in such an emotional frame of mind caused me to have physical symptoms that several doctors diagnosed as rheumatoid arthritis. Finally, specialists at the renowned Scott and White Memorial Hospital in Temple, Texas, told me my condition was progressing so rapidly that, within a matter of months, I would be totally disabled.

I couldn't bear the thought of returning home and having my mother support me and my three children. She had worked hard all her life, and asking her to take responsibility for us was an unthinkable prospect!

At this time I was working for Stanley Home Products and making $10 or $12 for each sales demonstration party. I had to give three Stanley parties every day if I simply hoped to make ends meet. I realized that in order to be successful, I had to leave my personal problems at home, so I decided that no matter how I felt, I would go in there with a smile. As I succeeded in my career, my health improved, until finally all symptoms of rheumatoid arthritis disappeared. The doctors continued to insist that I was simply in a remission and that my arthritis would someday return. So far they've been dead wrong. I think those physical symptoms were induced by my extreme emotional stress and stopped when I took control of my attitude!

You see—the funny thing about putting on a happy face is that if you do it again and again, pretty soon that happy face is there to stay. It becomes the real you. I discovered that by maintaining a cheerful attitude during those Stanley parties, my problems seemed to go away, one by one. Conversely, if I had allowed myself to stay depressed, I wouldn't have done a good job, and I wouldn't have made enough in sales commissions. Then I really would have had compounded problems. Someone once said, "A man is about as happy as he makes up his mind to be." And I believe that!

It has always been my philosophy that a salesperson should never discuss personal problems with customers. I give our Consultants two suggestions regarding this belief: number one, mentally "turn off" your problems before going to a skin-care class, and number two, when you enter that door, enter with enthusiasm. When people ask, "How are you?" they don't really want to know. They don't care that your husband has lost his job, your children have chicken pox, or your water heater just broke down. Don't inflict your troubles on them. If you do, it will cause a negative atmosphere that can only destroy rapport. It's better never to let anyone know you have a care in the world. When I came through the door at each of those early Stanley parties, little did anyone know that I had left a myriad of problems at home. When the hostess says, "Hello, how are you?" say "Wonderful! And how are you?"—even if you have to say it through clenched teeth! Besides, if you act enthusiastic and happy, do a good job, and come out of that skin-care class with $200 in sales—believe me, you will be enthusiastic and happy!

It's important to realize that nobody is highly motivated every day. There are times when even the most enthusiastic person will wake up feeling depressed. And yes, I have days when I wake up and just don't feel "with it." I might be tired, or I might have something on my schedule that is distasteful. Those are the times when I *generate* enthusiasm. One step that helps me do this is to read good motivational books and listen to motivational tapes. I especially like to listen to tapes while I'm dressing and while I'm driving to the office and back home. It's a wonderful way to keep from wasting precious time.

Singing also seems to cheer people up. I've told you about the songs we sometimes sing at Mary Kay meetings. Some people have criticized us for this, because they think songs are silly. But we have found that when people are in a negative frame of mind, songs have a wonderful effect on their morale. I believe that is the same reason churches begin their services with hymns. As a young mother, I remember driving to church with three small children squabbling in the backseat. Sometimes I felt I had lost my religion by the time we got there! I certainly was in no mood to be in church. But after singing two or three hymns, I felt a lot better; I was ready to absorb my pastor's message.

At the beginning of our unit meetings, we also have a time when Consultants tell about their successes of the previous week. We encourage each person to stand up and enthusiastically tell the group something wonderful that happened to her. Even if you *have* had a bad week, after hearing a couple of dozen people talk about how well they've done, you begin to think, "If they can do it, I can do it, too." A happy face and a happy attitude are always an inspiration to others.

Of course, there are times when it takes a special effort to put on a happy face. My beloved husband Mel Ash passed away on Monday, July 7, 1980. Mel had smoked for forty-seven years. For the last ten of those years, I begged, cajoled, reasoned, and pleaded to get him to stop. He often tried, but in a few hours he would say, "Mary Kay, I *can't* stop; I just can't." Then one evening I was reading an article about how you could actually get lung cancer from living with an inveterate smoker and inhaling secondary smoke. I turned the magazine over on the coffee table, knowing full well that his curiosity would make him look the next morning to see what I had been reading. Sure enough, he picked up that article. Simultaneously, he saw a television commercial for a clinic specializing in helping to kick the smoking habit. Because he loved me and cared about me, he enrolled in the program and five days later stopped cold! For the next five years he never touched another cigarette. But it wasn't soon enough; the damage had already been done. We only knew of his inoperable lung cancer for seven weeks before his death.

The day after Mel's death, all our staff and the local Directors and Consultants were scheduled to leave Dallas for a conference in St. Louis. All these people dearly loved Mel, and I held the funeral Tuesday afternoon so that they could attend.

Because of Mel's illness, I had not planned to attend the St. Louis conference. But more than 7,500 Directors and Consultants were gathering from throughout the Midwest, and so I went to St. Louis on the following Friday. I knew that many women would be spending a good deal of money to travel to that conference, and I felt an obligation not to let them down. These meetings are supposed to be joyful, inspirational times, and so even though I was grief-stricken, I made certain that I generated a positive attitude for everyone present. I went out in front of that large audience and I did my best to project the happiness I felt for them, rather than the sorrow I felt for myself. I knew that my mood would influence everyone there, and I wanted them to have a positive experience.

I kept thinking of Jackie Kennedy Onassis, and how courageous she was when her husband was assassinated. The whole world praised her for her courage. She wouldn't allow herself the luxury of breaking down, and her strength had a tremendous impact on many other people. Later, when they faced tragedies in their own lives, they remembered how she had kept her head up, not crying in public, and they knew that they could do it, too. In my own small way, I was trying to do the same thing at our gathering. Since then, I've received countless letters from women telling me that the fact I was able to put on a happy face during my grief had inspired them to do the same thing when they've suffered a tragedy in their own lives.

Life has many sad moments, but living must always go on. Just a few days before our 1978 Seminar, another tragedy occurred. Sue Vickers, one of our most beautiful and talented National Sales Directors, was kidnaped in the parking lot of a Dallas shopping center and murdered. Sue was known in our company as "Miss Enthusiasm," and her warmth and "Go-Give" spirit were an inspiration to everyone who knew her. Her death was a tremendous tragedy to all of us.

Sue was scheduled to give a speech at the 1978 Seminar. Among her notes for the presentation, she had written,

> Be Somebody—Be Great.
>
> I Can Do All Things Through Christ Who Strengthens Me.
>
> Do Big Things—Don't Give Up!
>
> Be an Inspiration to Others!
>
> What the World Needs Is a Word of Good Cheer!
>
> Enthusiasm! Love! And Laughter!

These thoughts clearly illustrate the kind of person Sue was. Her senseless death was a great loss to me, as well as to everyone else who knew her, but we put on our happy faces, dedicated the Seminar to Sue, and went on as scheduled. I'm sure that's the way Sue would have wanted it.

It's easy to smile and be enthusiastic when everything is going along perfectly in your life. Under ideal circumstances, anyone can project cheerfulness, but the real test of a champion is being able to put on a happy face when deep down you're suffering with a serious personal problem.

One such champion is Rena Tarbet, mother of three, and a National Sales Director—so positive and cheerful, you would never know that she's had two mastectomies and reconstructive surgery.

Rena has an attitude that is an inspiration to everyone. She's so enthusiastic! She loves life, she loves her work, and she never lets illness stop her. She often tells a wonderful story about something that happened while she was waiting to be tested at M. D. Anderson Hospital and Tumor Research Institute at Houston. She had waited much of the day and was next in line, when the head nurse announced to the remaining patients that the doctor would be unable to see anyone else until the following afternoon. Rena had a Mary Kay workshop to conduct the next day. So she went up to the physician and told him she had to be in Dallas the following afternoon.

"Is there any reason why you couldn't see just one more patient today, doctor?" she asked. He thought for a moment, and because of her smiling attitude, consented to her request.

When she first told me the story, she beamed. "I used the same selling technique you taught me," she said, "the one where we ask a woman, 'Is there any reason why you couldn't be a hostess for a skin-care class?'"

After her workshop, Rena told me what the doctor had found. She would have to receive chemotherapy and radiation treatments for several months, and it was likely that she would lose all her hair. But she just smiled and said, "Guess I'll have to get myself a really pretty wig, Mary Kay."

As I listened to Rena talk so positively, I admired her serene and cheerful expression. I had to fight to hold back my tears, and it took everything I had to take my own advice and put on a happy face. Yet, as I looked at Rena's happy face, I knew I could do no less.

Recently, she told another gathering that her spirits were high and her determination was unyielding. She shared with us a quote from Montaigne's *Essays*: "The value of life lies not in the length of days but in the use we make of them. A man may live long yet get little from life. Whether you find satisfaction in life depends not on your tale of years but on your will."

As Rena spoke those words, I looked at her and I was filled with pride. I knew she had truly discovered the meaning of life. I gave her a big hug and, thankfully, only my happy emotions came pouring out.

After undergoing six years of chemotherapy, Rena's cancer has been in remission for many years. She has served as an inspiration to all of us.

7

God First, Family Second, Career Third

OVER THE YEARS, I have found that everything seems to work out if you have your life in the proper perspective: God first, family second, and career third. I truly believe the growth of Mary Kay Cosmetics has come about because the first thing we did was to take God as our partner. If we had not done that, I don't believe we would be where we are today. I believe He has blessed us because our motivation is right. He knows I want women to become the beautiful creatures He created, and to *use* the wonderful God-given talents that lie within each of us.

I've found that when you just let go and place yourself in God's hands, everything in your life goes right. When you try to do everything alone and rely on yourself, you begin to make major errors.

None of us at Mary Kay works alone. My son Richard is a brilliant administrator, an outstanding corporate planner, and is recognized as one of today's bright financial geniuses. Nevertheless, not even he can look at computer printouts or market surveys and truly predict the future. Yet it often appears that he has done just that. I believe we have found success because God has led us all the way. I can't tell you how many times we've needed something only to have it miraculously appear at our door.

Our experience with hexachlorophene is one small example. Several years ago, this was a highly regarded and widely used ingredient we included in the formula for our body lotion. We made the decision that hexachlorophene may have some shortcomings, and so we removed it from our line and destroyed approximately nineteen thousand bottles of lotion. Shortly after this action, the Food and Drug Administration outlawed the ingredient and ordered manufacturers to destroy all supplies containing hexachlorophene. Had we not made the proper decision when we did, we, like other manufacturers, could have incurred a loss of hundreds of thousands of dollars.

Richard's reaction to this miraculous timing was, "Our scientists knew these things were going to happen, so they acted accordingly." But *nobody* can predict the future, and nobody knows what the FDA is going to do from one day to the next. There were undoubtedly some recent studies done that our scientists had read. But for whatever reason, we had removed that chemical by the time the edict was issued, and thus we avoided a costly problem.

But a business consists of millions of small decisions, not just the big ones. Often it's the little, daily decisions—the ones you make hour by hour—that mean the difference between success and failure. And I feel that God put His protective arm around us and guided us to the right path.

Although I believe that God has been instrumental in the growth of our business, I'm careful to remember that we *are* a business and that I must avoid preaching to our people. After all, as a company with so many associates, we are represented by every faith and denomination. Because of our philosophy—God first, family second, career third—we seem to attract spiritually strong people who agree that God and family should be preeminent in their lives. I never try to impose my personal religious beliefs on anyone. I do let it be known, however, that God is a very important part of my life.

I am also quite vocal regarding my belief in strong family ties. I stress that no matter how successful you are in your career, if you lose your family in the process of attaining that success, then you have failed. Money is not worth sacrificing your family. A career is a means to an end—a means by which you can provide comforts and security for your family—but what you accomplish in your career is not an end in itself. Unfortunately, some people become so consumed with their work that they lose sight of what's really important in life.

When I first started supporting my family as a Stanley dealer, I only had room for three things: God, family, and career. I had no social life. Every waking hour was geared to my three children, my work, and my church. I didn't know what it was like to go to a movie or to have dinner out with a friend. My entire day was planned around the children's schedule. I got up at five o'clock so that I could do my housework before they arose. Then I gave them a good breakfast and got them off to school. After they were gone, I left, too—for my first party. I'd have another party in the early afternoon, and then I would make certain to be home to greet my children when they came home from school. I gave them their dinner and got them ready for bed. Then at seven o'clock, I would leave for my evening party. My housekeeper would have them asleep long before I got back. It worked out fine. I was able to have my cake and eat it too, because I was a working mother who still made time to be with her children. I was just sure to thank God for my high energy level!

One of the things I was able to do for the children was to take the family to Galveston, Texas, for summer vacations. While at the Gulf, we stayed in a beachfront room at the Galvez Hotel. I would take the children down to the beach each morning and stay as long as I could without getting sunburned. Then I would go upstairs to our room, sit at the window, and keep an eye on them. At lunch, I'd take them to get a hot dog or sandwich, and after they had eaten, they would go back to the beach. I went back to my window. Because of my fair skin, the beach was not the place I would have selected for myself, but *my* vacation was watching the children enjoy themselves.

Those two weeks in Galveston were the only time I didn't work. The rest of the year, my life was strictly God, family, and work, work, work. Once I heard Dr. Joyce Brothers say that being a workaholic isn't all bad; it simply means that you're totally committed. I would like to think she's right, because I certainly would have fallen into that category.

It was necessary for me to work every night in order to make ends meet. But thanks to Richard, some of the neighbors didn't take too kindly to my late hours. By the time we had moved to Dallas, I was making a good living and we had moved into a nice neighborhood. We had a two-story brick house with a little front porch and a front lawn with a large tree. By that time, I also had a housekeeper who was supposed to tuck the children in bed after I left. But apparently she would tuck them in and go to her room. At any rate, Richard would wait until the house was quiet, go out on the small balcony adjoining his room, climb down the adjacent tree, and sit on the curb waiting for his mother to come home.

He loves to tell this story: "Mary Kay never could understand why the neighbors didn't like her. They would see me sitting on that curb and ask, 'Where's your mother?' And I would answer, 'She's at a party.'" He never seemed to mention that the "party" was a Stanley party—and my work!

Although I worked long, hard hours while the children were growing up, I arranged my schedule so that I was there when they needed me. I made myself available to help with their homework, and they knew that I would drop anything to discuss a serious problem. One of the nicest things about my flexible hours was that I could always be home to give my tender loving care if one of the children was ill. My family was the only thing I ever let interfere with my work.

Employers need to understand that children *are* parents' priorities. I've seen people with nine-to-five jobs come to work when they had a very sick child at home. In my opinion, their employers would have been better off telling them to stay home and take care of the child. There's just no way parents can keep their minds on work when worried about a sick child. And you notice that I use the word *parents*. If you're a single parent like I was, you must carry the full load. But if both parents are present (even after a "friendly divorce"), employers must let fathers and mothers share in these responsibilities.

Your responsibilities also extend to other family members. My husband Mel was seriously ill with cancer for seven weeks before he died. For the first two weeks after we discovered his illness, we really didn't know whether or not it was terminal. But I sent a message to my office that I would not be in until Mel was better. I knew they all understood how I feel about family coming before business. And for those seven weeks, I did not once go into the office. My staff sent home my paperwork, and when Mel was sleeping, I would go to my desk and do whatever seemed urgent.

Before any of this happened, I had been looking forward to giving a speech to the General Federation of Women's Clubs that was meeting in St. Louis, June 1980. The speech had been arranged a year in advance, and there would be several thousand women attending from all over the country. I was excited about having the chance to share the Mary Kay philosophy with so many women. But I would have had to leave Mel for two days, and I just couldn't do that. So Dalene White, one of our National Sales Directors, went to St. Louis in my place and did an excellent job of representing our company.

I'm aware that most companies expect their employees to put their jobs before all else in their lives. Yes, I know that a person can become so wrapped up in his or her work that the family is neglected. But I don't see how anyone could expect work to come before family in a time of real need.

I'm told that it's unusual for a company to encourage such a philosophy, but we've been doing it ever since our business began. As I've said, when you put God first, your family second, and your career third, everything seems to work. Out of that order, nothing much seems to work. When you get to the bottom line, it doesn't matter how much money you've made, how big your house is, or how many cars you own. For on that day when God calls you to accept your relationship with Jesus Christ, nothing else matters. Each of us will come to that day—and we must ask ourselves whether or not our lives have been meaningful.

8

The Story of One Career Woman and Many Hats

WE HAVE WITNESSED a great social change in the past few decades. In 1963, 32 percent of all married couples included a wife in the labor force; in 1983, 51 percent of all married couples included wives who worked outside the home. Two out of every three young women leaving school now move smoothly and efficiently into the workplace. In fact, it's estimated that by the end of the early 1990s the number of women-owned businesses will surpass the number employed by the *Fortune* 500. In 1993 the National Foundation of Women Business Owners reported 4.5 million women own their own business.

Our daughters and granddaughters do not think of *supplementing* their lives with a career, because having a career and being a woman are now seen as naturally equal parts of the same role. When I began working, being a young career woman meant that I had four separate roles: I was first a wife, a mother, and a homemaker; then I was a businesswoman. Each role made many demands on my time and extracted a great deal of energy. Women of that era were expected to wear a lot of hats. A woman could be as much of a breadwinner as her husband, but she also had to be a housekeeper, laundress, chauffeur, teacher, nurse, errand boy, social director, house maintenance staff, and *bread baker*. I often said, a career woman in those days needed her own "wife"!

A woman seeking a career back then found little support from anybody else. We were told that in order to work outside the home, we had to make sacrifices—even compromises—if we were to keep it all together. A man could go to work in the morning, kiss his wife and children goodbye, and give his full attention to his career. But we women were told that if we wanted a toehold in that big ocean called business, we had to be sure the beds were made and the shirts were ironed first. The burden of family success rested solely on female shoulders. If you wanted to work back then, it seemed that your only "excuse" was if you were widowed, divorced, or never married. Even so, the attitude of both men and women was that you were simply taking a job until you could find something better (namely, a new husband).

Thank heaven times have changed! There are a few hardheaded holdouts, but most people now realize that women (just like men) need the growth, challenge, and financial independence a career can offer. The best part is that anything goes now—you may work outside your home part-time, fulltime, or "no" time. The choice is yours.

A change in social attitudes has also brought many timesaving and woman-saving innovations. It's easy to take such things for granted, but I remember when there were no highquality day-care centers, extended public-school hours, fastfood restaurants, permanent-press clothing, dishwashers, or microwaves. The logistics of managing your home and your career are made far easier by these changes. For example, if you are a mother today, it is much easier for you to find loving, professional care for your children. We have even changed in our attitudes about what constitutes "successful parenting." We have come to see that it's more important to talk to your daughter than to starch her cotton pinafore. It's more important to listen to your son than to put creases in his trousers. The child psychologists tell us we should teach our children to take care of their own personal chores as soon as

they can. That will make them stronger and more independent, and it will let you be a much more efficient household
manager.

And men have changed, too. Women have yet to reach
financial parity in most offices, but as power moves to
younger executives, that too will change. A survey of busi-
nessmen, ages twenty-five to sixty-five, concluded that men
forty-five and under were far more likely to think of women
as social and professional equals. In addition, these younger
men were much more inclined to help a woman up the corporate ladder. In the past, men seemed threatened by a professional woman. They liked their wives and lovers to be home-
bound and out of the workplace. Some cynics say the change
has come about because it now takes two incomes to maintain
a family. But whatever the reason, their acceptance of our
place in business means that most modern men now share in
both the joyous duties of childrearing and the mundane
duties of housework. Men love their children as much as
women do, and once they learned how rewarding it is to help
mold young lives, they *wanted* in on the act. Many men are
also helping in the chores around the house. Let's face it,
nobody, male *or* female, really *likes* cleaning the bathroom. But
when a man and a woman share a household and share the
advantages of a career, then they should also share the little
tasks of daily maintenance. That gives them both more time
for children, career, and each other.

My purpose in this chapter is to share with you some of
the techniques that have helped me balance my home and my
office. I believe that the lessons I have learned are applicable
for many different career women—married, single, widowed,
or divorced. It's not possible, and I think not necessary, for me
to write a book giving rules for any combination of factors that
may pertain to each individual reader. For example, I can't say,
"If you're divorced, work part-time, and have no children,
then you should do this," or "Do this if you're married to a
fabulous husband and father who helps you fold the laundry

and pack lunches for the children." (By the way, ladies, if you have that one, hold on to him!) All I can do is tell you my story, just as I lived it, and hope that after reading it, you may apply some of my solutions to your own set of circumstances.

I think the most exhausting time of my life was when I was raising my three children, working as a Stanley dealer, and going to college. I had been married for ten years and I had always dreamed of becoming a doctor. My sales career seemed established, and I thought, "*Now* is the time!" This was back in the days when it was considered a waste of time for a married woman to go to college. Professors would look you square in the eye and tell you that you were taking up a spot that could be filled by a younger *man*. So when I was in school, I tried to conceal the fact that I was a wife and mother. I dressed like a student, even down to my bobbysocks. I wore my wedding ring on a chain around my neck, and I never mentioned my three children at home.

I usually had classes in the morning and a Stanley party in the afternoon. When I got home, I'd clean house, wash diapers, cook meals, and so on. But there was still a terrific problem: after all that work, I was too tired to study. Sometimes I would go to bed shortly after the children did and set my alarm for three o'clock in the morning. I'd get up, drink some coffee, and study until the children woke up around seven o'clock. Finally, I could no longer keep up the pace. I was about to have a nervous breakdown, because I was burning the candle at both ends and right up the middle!

It is strange how things always seem to work out for the best. I was killing myself with my scientific studies when I was given a three-day-long aptitude test. When the dean called me into her office to discuss the results, she told me that my scores in science, though good, were far surpassed by my scores in other areas—such as persuasion. She highly recommended that I change my courses to marketing and pursue a career as a buyer or saleswoman. She pointed out that in four years I could probably get a good-paying job as a professional salesperson or buyer for a large department store. (Of course, she didn't know that I was *already* pursuing a "part-time" sales career that was supporting my children and paying my college tuition.)

Furthermore, she argued that becoming a doctor would require two years of pre-med study, four years of medical school, and then an internship of a year or so. This meant that getting into medical practice could take almost ten years. She felt I should opt for the shorter route to a good-paying career.

Her words didn't make my decision, but they did make sense. I added them to other conclusions I had reached and decided to drop out of college and work full-time selling Stanley products. Once the choice was made, I was still working long hours—at both my sales job and my *family* job—but my schedule wasn't quite so hectic.

I began working on a straight commission basis, and this was an advantage. It meant that I could work *my* time, not company time. Many women do work strict office hours, but I knew that I couldn't raise my family and sit at a desk from nine to five each day. I needed the flexibility my sales job offered, so I could be with my children when they needed me. I arranged my Stanley parties so I was home after school to greet my children, prepare their dinner, and give them my full attention.

Wearing many hats can take its toll, but still, it is something you can accomplish. I found that the best way to do this is to become organized. You must decide your priorities, divide your time accordingly, and share what duties you can with others. If you have a loving and helping family, that's where you start. But you should also consider the financial advantages to "subcontracting" elements of your work. Some people like doing laundry and scrubbing floors. I don't. I found that I usually wasted time and energy that could be put to more productive use—namely, making sales. So as soon as I could afford it, I hired a housekeeper. For me, it was a necessity—not a luxury. But some people find this too great an expense, and others do not like losing their sense of privacy. If this is true for you, consider employing a cleaning service to give your house a good weekly once-over. You may find that you actually save money because your time will be managed more efficiently.

After my divorce, I quickly learned that being a single career woman with children meant that I *really* had to learn time management. It helped to remember my priorities: God first, family second, career third. I think that many women make the mistake of becoming caught up in too many outside activities. While community and civic projects are very important, I do not believe that they should be done at the expense of our families. If joining the PTA is important for your child's sake, then I'm all for it. But if it's just a social occasion for you, then perhaps you should eliminate it. A mother working outside of the home must decide how much time she has and which activities she can afford.

On January 6, 1966, I married Mel Ash. This change in my life presented a totally different set of joys and challenges. I met Mel through a mutual friend when my dream company was only two years old. He had built his own successful business; as Mary Kay Cosmetics grew, so did his involvement with its goals and objectives. Shortly before he died, Mel remarked, "I'm a father with a hundred thousand daughters." And that's how he truly felt about the women of our company. Often, observers saw him standing in the background while I stood center stage. But what few people knew was that many times, Mel was quietly and efficiently solving problems that others may have not even recognized.

I'll never forget the snowstorm in Chicago. We were in the last session of a three-day meeting for two thousand Consultants and Directors when an unexpected blizzard closed all traffic in and out of the city. Even if we could have made it out the front door of the hotel, we couldn't have gone anywhere from there. We were literally snowbound. At the end of the conference we told the audience of our plight, and that they could check back into their rooms. We made arrangements for the company to pick up the bill for dinner in the hotel dining room, and we scheduled impromptu workshops for the duration of the storm.

But many of the women had attended the conference on a very tight budget and had no money for an extended stay. And they certainly couldn't spend the night in the hotel lobby. For the next few hours, everything was very chaotic. Women were trying unsuccessfully to call home, they were wandering around the hotel, and some were even in tears because they didn't know how they could pay for extra meals and lodging. But people adapt; and after we got the workshops going, things began to settle down. In fact, over the next couple of days, it even became a party. It was only much later that I learned what had really happened during those first few hours. Using his unlimited hotel credit, Mel had been quietly moving through the crowd, finding women who were distressed and lending them money. Mind you, he kept no records of these transactions. No names and no dollar amounts. He simply gave the money to any woman who said she needed it. I knew nothing of this until we were back in Dallas. Suddenly Mel began receiving scores of letters containing money. Naturally I asked, "Mel, what's going on here? Why are all these women sending you money?"

"Oh nothing," he would say. And then he'd open another batch of envelopes containing checks or money.

It was much later that I learned the whole story—and not from Mel. He was much too modest to have boasted of his generosity. That's just the kind of man he was!

Many people have been delighted by another example of Mel's generosity—my Thursday gifts. We were married on a Thursday, and so from the very beginning, Thursday was a special day for us. *Every* Thursday for the fourteen years of our marriage, Mel brought me a gift. Depending upon his mood or his financial situation, the gifts ranged from a flower to a piece of peanut brittle to a diamond. But no matter what, every single Thursday I would come home to find a gift-wrapped package and a beautiful, personally chosen greeting card. And he was just as generous with compliments, too. Every morning he told me how beautiful I looked—and you *know* that wasn't true. Like lots of women, I often went to bed looking like Elizabeth Taylor and woke up looking like Charles de Gaulle! Of course, I wanted to live up to his compliment, so every morning, I was out of bed before Mel was awake, trying to look beautiful for him. I remember how I always wanted to get my makeup on before he put his spectacles on!

Even though he was devoted to Mary Kay Cosmetics, Mel was from the old school: he didn't like it when my work interfered with "his" time. He liked to call himself "the chairman of the chairman of the board." When I came home at night, he wanted me to be somebody who was thinking only of him; because I loved him, I respected that.

It took me sixteen minutes every evening to drive home from my office, and in that time I would have to take off my chairman-of-the-board hat and replace it with my Mel Ash's–wife hat. Mel wanted me to be home at seven o'clock on the dot, and this took a bit of adjusting on my part. After five, I found that the office would become quiet and I could get down to some serious thinking. Often I would become so involved, that I would forget to watch the clock. If I was a minute late, Mel would begin to worry. So I made a special effort to leave the office on time—no matter what. I did this because I knew how important it was for Mel, and his feelings were very important to me. Of course, by seven o'clock, he would have quite an appetite, so I became an expert in the art of "quick and delicious meals." I'd usually ask the housekeeper to set the table and leave a salad in the refrigerator or a casserole in the oven. Sometimes, in a pinch, I even got good at fixing up those frozen dinners so they tasted like homemade.

I remember one of our Beauty Consultants telling me that when she got home late and didn't have anything for dinner, she'd throw an onion in a pot of boiling water, and it would smell like something good was cooking. That wonderful aroma made her husband feel that a delicious meal was under way. In the meantime, she'd pull something out of the freezer. While some people might not appreciate what she did, it kept her husband happy—and that's all that really mattered to her. Today when a career woman arrives home late from work, she is more likely to take her husband (or kids) by the hand and say, "Come on, Honey. We're cooking something together." (That is, if her modern husband hasn't already prepared something himself!)

Mel also liked me to sit with him for a few hours each evening and watch television or talk. Perhaps it was the workaholic in me that often made it hard to relax and do nothing. And I must confess that there were times when I thought, "What a waste of time it is to sit in front of this television set, when I could be getting something done!" But I loved Mel, and I knew that this time together was important to him.

Once in a while, I tried to watch television with one eye and read the day's accumulation of mail with the other. But Mel felt that I was using "his time," and he resented it. Finally, I changed my schedule. I'd still go to bed when he did, but I'd get up at five o'clock each morning and start my dictation. That way I could complete my correspondence and paperwork without Mel ever feeling I was infringing upon his time. Then at seven-thirty, he would get up, and I would change hats and become Mel Ash's wife once again. I didn't mind the switch, because I felt I was making my own choices. And I think that's what a loving, open relationship is all about.

It takes a great deal of time and energy for a woman to really care for a family and build a career at the same time. If she's going to survive, she must choose her hats wisely, learn when and how to balance them, and discard those which distract from her personal priorities.

9

The Career Woman and Her Family

Do you know how a Mary Kay Consultant calls her family to dinner?

"Come on, kids, let's get in the car."

Do you know what a Mary Kay Director makes for her family's Sunday dinner?

Reservations.

The public perception of "family" used to be a husband, a wife, three kids, and a dog. Daddy went to work, Mother kept house, and the kids played with the dog. Now we recognize that families come in many combinations and include many age groups and relationships. Family can mean you and a child, or you and a parent—the specific details do not change the rules. If you have a career outside your home, the first rule is that you must coordinate your needs with those of your family members. Family is a team project.

In some families it is a fact of life that everyone—father, mother, grandparent, and teenager—has a job outside the home. The whole team thinks nothing of pitching in and helping run the household. Of course, if your family consists of you and your cat, you probably have a pretty easy time getting the team to go along with you. But for some women, taking on additional job responsibilities means a change in the way the family has been operating. If this is true for you, a good start is to plan the transition very carefully.

Thankfully, a woman who keeps her wits about her doesn't have to choose between family and career—she can have both. All it requires is that you set priorities and get yourself organized.

I once heard someone say, "To know oneself is to disbelieve in utopia." But if utopia comes at all, it doesn't just come automatically. *You have to make it happen.*

Take a few moments from each busy day to think about how your family might be feeling about your role as a career woman. Perhaps after spending years as a full-time wife or mother, you suddenly decide to branch out into the business world. That's wonderful; I applaud your spirit! But the truth is, your husband or children may not accept this change as easily as you would like. *You're* excited about your new challenges, but *they* may see your job as competition for your attention. Even if you have always had a career, sometimes professional advancement will make new and greater challenges on your time and energy. Your family may begin to feel short-changed and show some resentment toward your work. You are the only one who will be able to judge if, or when, such negative circumstances are occurring. But in my opinion, no amount of success is worth sacrificing the relationship you have with your family. Conversely, the woman who gathers the support of her family is much more likely to succeed in both personal and professional roles. So what are you to do? Turn down a promotion? Stay home when you really want to get a job? Absolutely not! Like any other human relations problem, this one can be solved if you consider the feelings and opinions of the people around you. And I think the first step is to help your family see how your career will benefit *everyone.*

The most obvious benefit may be financial. In these economic times, everyone can use some extra income. But perhaps a more significant benefit is the way a career can make you feel about yourself and, in turn, about everyone around you. Meeting new challenges is intellectually and emotionally stimulating. It gives you a whole new perspective on your skills as an individual. Many of our new Consultants find themselves achieving things they never dreamed possible. One result of this new self-awareness is that it usually causes a woman to completely reevaluate her appearance. We have found that if a woman had not previously taken care of her personal appearance, having a career outside the home gives her a whole new outlook. She wants to be as well groomed as the other Consultants, and soon she is not only making her face prettier, but she is doing something a little different about her hair, her nails, and her clothing as well. It doesn't take her family long to notice her new look, and we've found that everyone is pleased with the transformation. That's because such changes are more than surface. If a person feels proud of his or her appearance, that pride develops into confidence, and that confidence leads to new achievements. The first step toward getting people to respect you is to respect yourself.

We believe so strongly that it's essential for a career woman to have the support of her family that we do everything we can to help her get it. When a Director attends New Director Development in Dallas, for example, we send a note to her family thanking them for their support. We also invite husbands to attend workshops and seminars where they are introduced to Mary Kay Cosmetics and the special challenges and rewards our company can offer. Maybe it's because I remember my own son sitting on the curb and talking to the neighbors, but we want each family member to understand what the Consultant is doing when she's out conducting a Mary Kay skin-care class.

At one Seminar, every husband received a button that read, "She's Fantastic!" Then when anyone would ask, "Who's fantastic?" the Consultant's husband could answer, "My wife!"

Those buttons really built enthusiasm, and they resulted in many husbands finding recruits and customers for their wives. One year we gave our visiting husbands a bumper sticker that read, "Ask Me About My Wife's Career." When a Consultant's husband attends such workshops and seminars, he invariably leaves feeling that anything those other women can do, *she* can do better.

At Mary Kay Cosmetics, we also respect the special needs of women with children. Many of our Consultants cite the flexibility of their work hours as one of the most important aspects of their careers. Because what does a nine-to-five mother do when little Johnny has a 103-degree fever and she *has* to be at work that day? If she is married, her husband can usually help, but if she is widowed or divorced, she can be in a real pinch. For emergencies such as this, we have what we call our "dovetail system." If one of our Consultants is ill or has a family emergency, she just calls another Consultant who will take her place and conduct the scheduled skin-care class.

Many career women feel guilty about working because they can't spend as much time as they would like with their children. And after a long, hard day, they may be too tired to expend the level of energy it takes to run the household and keep up with all of the children's activities. I think this is where you must set priorities and recognize that the quality of the time you spend with your child is far more important than the quantity. Just being in the proximity of your children does not automatically make you a successful parent. You can sit in the same room with a child and never give him or her a moment's attention. In fact, a parent who's with the children all day long sometimes gets the screaming-meemies by five o'clock and ends up shouting, "Don't ask me that question again!" That's not being a good parent—that's just being there. I found that when I was away from my children for a few hours each day, I was a better mother than when I was home all day long. The children seemed to appreciate me more, and I know that I was more patient with them.

Setting priorities also means that you may need to delegate (or even forget) some of those household duties that take up precious time. This is where a housekeeper or cleaning service can be of great help. In the next chapter, I'll talk a little more about the "fiscal wisdom" of hiring a housekeeper, but even if you decide to do your own housework—be realistic. You have just come home from a long and productive day of selling. Select those tasks that *really* must be done. If you must choose between two important activities, choose to talk to your children rather than to clean out your closets. Better yet, clean out the closets together and have your conversation while you work!

If you are a married career woman with a more traditional family structure, I believe it's essential that you gain your husband's support. Maybe your first sale will be to sell him on the correctness of your career choice. And if this is true for you, it's been my observation that *people will support that which they help to create*—so get him involved in your work. Mary Kay Consultants are independent business-women, and we have found that many of them involve their husbands in professional activities such as record keeping, bookkeeping, or deliveries. Many husbands also take care of the children while their wives are holding skin-care classes. One man recently wrote and thanked me for this involvement. He said that since his wife began her Mary Kay career, he had gotten to know his children and to appreciate more fully those responsibilities that he had formerly associated with "mothering."

Early in my Stanley sales career, I didn't have a husband to get involved, so I got my children involved instead. I used to put the money collected from each hostess into an envelope, and then when we finished our deliveries, I poured the contents out in the middle of the living-room carpet. The children would sit down and sort and count the money. They also helped in filling orders or making deliveries. We turned "Mother's work" into "everybody's work"—and fun work at that! My children learned the value of money, self-discipline, the importance of meeting deadlines and commitments, the importance of setting goals, and some math to boot. Of course, at the time, this seemed nothing more than common sense. But I have heard child psychologists list similar activities when instructing women in ways to balance a career and child rearing. Apparently the experts have concluded that we should take those routine jobs that everyone *must* do and turn them into fun activities your children will *want* to do.

While it's good to have your family involved in your career, you must be careful not to bring your problems home to them. Sometimes people make the mistake of discussing every little conflict at the dinner table, and this only serves to upset the family. For example, not long ago I received a harsh letter from the husband of one of our Directors. He listed all the things he believed were wrong with our operation, and just what he thought would solve every one of our problems. As it turned out, the *real* problem was that his wife had a habit of detailing every tiny thing that annoyed her. Naturally, he then took her side of every issue and blew the situation totally out of proportion.

I answered his letter, trying to soothe his feelings. A short time later, I spoke with his wife at a unit meeting.

"You're making the same mistake I used to make," I told her. "I used to tell Mel all about every little office problem that upset me, and he would roll them into a big ball and get mad at everyone who was hurting his dear, little wife."

She listened carefully and then said, "You know, Mary Kay, you're absolutely right. I *have* been bringing home little annoyances; and he *has* been rolling them up and magnifying them. Things aren't nearly as bad as he makes them out to be." Subsequently, she decided to stop telling him about her petty annoyances and focus instead on all of the good things that had been happening.

She later wrote and told me that everything has been resolved. It must be—I haven't heard another word from him and her unit is soaring!

Even if you are very involved with your career, I think it is a good idea to learn how to click it off like a television set. You must remember that members of your family are not as interested in your work as you are. It's fine to share interesting little tidbits, but keep office tensions at the office. Use the time with your family to share and enjoy *family business*. A smart career woman finds that taking time to *really be* with her family will allow each aspect of her life to flourish. You must consciously set aside certain hours of every day to devote to your loved ones.

Building a career can be extremely fulfilling. You will discover strengths and resolve weaknesses you never knew existed within yourself. But if you lose your family in the process, then I believe you will have failed. Success is so much more wonderful when you have someone to share it with. It's no fun to come home and count your money by yourself.

10

The $35,000 List

EARLY IN MY SALES CAREER, I heard a story that was to have a lasting effect upon me and the way I work. The subject was time management, and the story concerned Ivy Lee, a leading efficiency expert, and Charles Schwab, president of a then-small company called Bethlehem Steel.

Ivy Lee called on Charles Schwab and said to him, "I can increase your efficiency—and your sales—if you will allow me to spend fifteen minutes with each of your executives."

Naturally, Schwab asked, "What will it cost me?"

"Nothing," Lee said, "unless it works. In three months, you can send me a check for whatever you think it's worth to you. Fair enough?"

Schwab agreed, so Lee spent fifteen minutes with executives from the struggling young steel company and asked them to complete a single task. Every evening for the next three months, each executive was to make a list of the six most important things he had to do the next day. Finally, the executive was to rank the items in their order of importance.

"Each morning, begin with the first item on the list," she told them, "and scratch it off when it's finished. Just work your way right down those six items. If you don't get something finished, it goes on the next day's list."

At the end of the three-month trial, efficiency and sales

had increased to such an extent that Schwab sent Lee a check for $35,000. Now that's still a lot of cash for such a small amount of work, but in today's money, $35,000 would probably be the equivalent of $350,000!

I was very impressed with this story. I thought that if such a list was worth S35,000 to Charles Schwab, it was worth $35 to me. So as I pondered the moral, I took an old envelope out of my purse and wrote down the six most important things I had to do the next day. And I have continued making that "$35,000 list" every single day of my life.

Everybody has been told to make a list, but this story convinced me that such a tool could actually mean money in my pocket. So this list became my mechanism for keeping on track. It's so easy to bounce around on a busy day, looking at a thousand important tasks and never quite knowing where to begin. The list solves that for me. The list will force you to decide which tasks are actually the *most important,* and for that reason it's essential to keep the list short and sweet. Don't be overzealous and put down seventeen things that must be done, because you'll look at that number and think, "I can't possibly do all this." Six is an amount easily managed. And if you reach a point where you can accomplish them all with ease—consider tackling bigger tasks!

Most important, you must go through the physical motions of writing it down on paper. It's too easy to run the list through your head and ignore or postpone something you wish to avoid. When it's on the list—it's for real.

Often I find I'm so busy that I don't have time to refer to my list, but by the time I glance at it again in the evening, I've usually accomplished most of the six. I think this is because sitting and writing the tasks reinforces them so that I subconsciously work toward my daily goals.

Another keystone to organizing my workday is organizing my desk. I hate to work at a cluttered desk, so every night I arrange my work so that completed projects are placed in one folder, work in process goes in another folder, materials to be reviewed go in a third folder, and so on. This way, I end each working day with a clean desk. When I arrive at the office the following morning, my secretary has organized my folders to coincide with my "$35,000 list" and I start to work, item by item. Instead of shuffling through everything and picking out the "goodies" (something we are all prone to do), I start with whatever's on top. No matter what. Even if it takes me two hours of research to answer the questions in that top letter, I don't go on until I've finished it. I continue, in order, until I work my way down to the bottom of the pile. I handle every piece of paper *only once*. I think this last point is very important; otherwise, you pick up a letter and say, "Gee, I don't know how to answer that; I'll have to think about it." You usually put the letter aside, pick it up a few hours later, and *still* don't know what to do with it. It's better to gather your research, go ahead, and make a decision. I see "shuffling papers" as a stumbling block for many ineffective managers. I believe in getting on with the work at hand. It seems to me that ineffective managers also spend more time worrying about something than it would take to actually accomplish the task. They worry their way through an entire day, when they should just "go ahead and do it." Often this happens because someone doesn't want to fail or look foolish. But remember, if you aren't willing to fail, you'll never succeed.

I try to organize my day so that I can save as much time as possible. One way to do this is by keeping tape recorders in my dressing room, kitchen, and car. In this way, I can use otherwise idle time by listening to motivational tapes and giving dictation. Another way I try to save time during the workday is to eat lunch in my office. I'm often invited to lunch by business associates, but I rarely accept these invitations. So-called "working lunches" can last until two or three in the afternoon, and sitting in a restaurant that long usually means that I eat too much and do not feel like working when I do get back to my office. The entire day has been lost. I prefer a quick, light lunch at my desk.

I guess that I've always been time-conscious. There are only twenty-four hours in a day, and all of my working life I've tried to get the most mileage out of those hours. Many years ago I heard someone remark that three early risings make an extra day. I thought about that, and said to myself, "If I get up at five o'clock for three mornings, I'll have an eight-day week. That's exactly what I've been looking for!"

Then I realized that if I got up early six times a week, I'd have a nine-day week! I also discovered how much more I could get done during those early-morning hours, when there were no phone calls or other interruptions. When I discovered how much I enjoyed a nine-day week, I decided to form my "Five O'Clock Club."

I invite everyone I know to get up at five o'clock and join the club, and it's amazing how many people with Mary Kay Cosmetics have decided to do just that. Of course, some people are truly at their best during the late hours, and for them functioning at five o'clock in the morning is impossible, but I always extend my invitation to every new Mary Kay Director. So many of them have written to tell me, "I've just joined your Five O'Clock Club, and I love it! I get so much done before my family gets up!"

In my speeches to professional and community groups, I often talk about the $35,000 list and my early-morning routine. If my audience is a class of prospective Mary Kay Directors, I'll ask how many want to join the Five O'Clock Club, and I'll always get a big show of hands.

Then I'll say, "Okay, that's great! One of these mornings, I'm going to call you at five-thirty and ask you to read me the six things on your list. Now, how many *still* want to join my club?" Surprisingly enough, they still raise their hands. (And I *have* been known to call!)

When you get up at such an early hour, it's sometimes hard to get yourself started. So I always suggest that when a woman gets up, she should make herself presentable for the rest of the day. This is *so* important for women who do not go to an office but who work, instead, from their homes. Getting dressed and putting on makeup lifts a woman's morale and puts her in a businesslike frame of mind. A woman who looks good feels good—and as a result, she will also "work good."

Once you're dressed, the first thing to do is start on your list of the day's six most important tasks. Begin with number one—and *don't procrastinate*.

Everyone has certain little tasks that are easier to avoid. For many Mary Kay Consultants, one such task is calling her customers, an essential element in our program of ensuring customer satisfaction. Two weeks after each sale, a Consultant is supposed to call the customer to make certain she's happy with her purchase. She will ask questions such as, "Are you using your Mary Kay skin care?" "Are you getting great results?" "Do you have any questions?" This is strictly a service call and a means of letting the customer know that we care about her. Let's face it, companies selling cosmetics over department-store counters don't call their customers. This contact helps us reinforce our unique level of service. Often a customer needs to be instructed once more in the proper use of a specific product. On rare occasions, a Consultant may need to pick up an item and exchange it for another formula, or even more rarely, refund the customer's money. Whatever the situation, when we *know* a customer's concerns, we can do something to resolve them.

All of this simply means that calling her customers is very important and should be at the top of every Consultant's list. But this happens to be one of those things people may avoid if they're afraid of rejection. It's easy to fear the task if you think someone will say, "Look, I don't have time to talk to you." Or worse, "I don't like those products you sold me." But such a fear is usually unfounded. Once a Consultant makes two or three calls and gets positive, enthusiastic feedback from her customers, she can't wait to get back on that phone.

I often tell our Consultants and Directors, "You are the only boss you have. And I want you to be the most demanding boss that you can be. If you really want to make a success of this business, then you must put yourself on a schedule. By eight-thirty every morning, you should have completed all your household duties. Then you should work from eight-thirty to five o'clock, allowing yourself a thirty-minute lunch break and a couple of ten-minute coffee breaks. Then at precisely five o'clock you're off work!" We have found that if a Consultant will spend as much time with her Mary Kay career as she would if she were working in an office, she can easily make twice as much money as any office job could pay. And we have Consultants and Directors who are proving this fact every single day.

Time is a salesperson's most valuable commodity. In fact, the way in which time is measured can mean the difference between success and failure. An excellent example is one of our Consultants who operates in the Southwest. She lives in a rural town with a population of 7,500. This small population would seem to limit her sales prospects, but our Consultant actually books classes within a 150-mile radius of her home. She is able to do this because she practices excellent time management. For example, when she organizes a class 100 miles away, she books another skin-care class in that vicinity for the same day. That way she doesn't waste time and money driving so far for a single appointment.

Ordinary people can utilize good time-management techniques and get great results. On the other hand, people who seem to have everything going for them can fail if they do not manage time. Often people in the latter group think they're working when in reality they're just worrying. Worrying about those letters they should have written. Worrying about those phone calls and sales they should have made. My advice has always been, "If you're going to waste a day, just waste the living daylights out of it. But if you're going to work, then *work.*" One intense hour is worth a dreamy day.

Perhaps this is why I have such little patience when people are not punctual. Recently I was asked to address a confer-

ence of businesswomen regarding ways they could more successfully organize and manage their careers. But the organizers of this event didn't even know how to manage the program. My speech was to have run from two until three
o'clock, and I had spent a great deal of effort efficiently packing as much information as I could into that time period. But
by two-fifteen on the afternoon of the speech, conference par-
ticipants were still coming into the auditorium and milling
around the registration table. The so-called organizers didn't
even know how to handle a group of a few hundred people!
Finally, they decided to begin the program anyway, and at
two-twenty-five my introduction was still in progress. When I
finally began to speak, the program was already half an hour
late. I have a little test I run when I am speaking before such
an audience—I look to see if anyone is interested enough to
take notes on the information I am providing. I looked out
into that crowd and I couldn't see a single pencil or pen. No
one was even slightly interested in learning the professional
tips or management shortcuts I was prepared to discuss. The
organizers had misled me into thinking this was a training
session, when apparently all the audience wanted was to be
entertained. So I departed from my written speech and began
telling them funny stories. They felt the speech was a success—because they had been entertained.

At Mary Kay Cosmetics, we feel we can't afford to waste
time in this manner. Every meeting has a useful purpose and
we *stick to the point* (inserting a little humor, of course). We also
are very strict about beginning and ending every meeting *on
time*. Every Monday thousands of Mary Kay unit meetings are
held across the country. With the responsibility for this many
sales professionals, we must set a good example—and we do.

Of course, you can use many of these same time-saving techniques when you organize the responsibilities you have at home.

For the first ten years of my career, I watched other
women succeed when I did not, because they were free to use
their time more productively. I used to say that as soon as I

could afford it, I was going to hire a housekeeper. If you have been telling yourself this same thing, let me give you one piece of good advice: you can't afford *not* to have a house-keeper. Hiring someone to free you from time-consuming household tasks can be one of the best career decisions you'll ever make. Remember, your time is the most important thing you have—make the most of it.

Do you realize that the president of the United States has the same amount of time that you have? But look at what he gets done each day! By ten in the morning—when most people are still on their second cup of coffee—chances are that he's telephoned several congressmen, signed seven bills into law, and had a press conference. He has to make these hours count. Each of us has twenty-four hours every day. But it's what you *do* with your twenty-four hours that makes the difference.

If you are serious about your career, I feel that you should not spend your twenty-four hours on tasks you could assign to someone else. I often tell our Beauty Consultants that one productive hour on the telephone can earn them enough money to pay for an entire day of housekeeping services. Don't worry about "ironing love" into your husband's collar, he probably doesn't even know about it (or care). He just wants a clean shirt ready when he needs it.

After people tell me they can't afford it, the second excuse I've heard is "I can't have a housekeeper. I'm too particular." That's no excuse. I'm so particular that I have to have the tow-els folded a certain way before they're put in the kitchen drawer. If someone folds them any other way, I want them refolded. But I taught my housekeeper how to do it for me, and you can teach someone how to do things for you. It might take a month to train someone, but it's time well spent. You must remember that your housekeeper is *also* a career woman, and she also wants to succeed in *her* job.

The important point is to get someone else to do those things that do not have to be done by you personally. One of the best things I ever did was to make a list of all the tasks that had to be done in a routine day. Then I checked off the ones that nobody else could do for me. These were the things I had to do, and I concentrated on doing them. I had someone else do all the rest. You are the only person who knows how this list will be tabulated. If you think it's important for your child that you lead a Cub Scout den—then by all means, do it. When you organize your time, you should first do those things that are truly important to you and your family. Then do what is important for your career. Anything after that is extra.

When I finally made the first decision to hire a house-keeper, I still had some doubts. I still thought of it as something I couldn't afford, but on sheer faith I put an ad in the weekend newspaper and waited for a response. Every time I started to think about paying a housekeeper, my heart would pound, because I really couldn't even afford to pay for the ad! I needed someone who could do *everything,* so I included all the requirements: cooking, cleaning, caring for three children, and so on. I ended the ad by stating the salary I could afford to pay; then I thought, "Anybody who's crazy enough to answer this ad is really asking for it!"

But on Sunday afternoon, a woman did apply. Mabel was a very lovely person and I was thrilled when she accepted the position. I thought, "How could I be so lucky?" My elation was short-lived when I remembered that she was to start work the following Monday morning—how on earth would I pay her?

Talk about being motivated! I had never booked so many parties, sold so much, or recruited as many people as I did that week. After all, I had to have enough extra for Mabel's salary. I made enough money to pay both of us, because she relieved me of so much of my housework. Every week thereafter, my goal was to earn enough on Monday to pay her salary on Friday. The rest of the week, whatever I earned was mine. It worked out so well that Mabel stayed with me for nine years.

Having a housekeeper has been so great for me that I must encourage other women to do the same. If you're still scrubbing floors, you've got to stop it! As one of our Directors once said, "I've been scrubbing the same spot in my house all my life—and it's still dirty." It's going to stay dirty, so get someone else to do that. Delegate your work. *Stop spending dollar time on penny jobs.*

Even if you aren't convinced that you need a housekeeper, it's still important to organize your house as you organize your career. Let me give you a tip that I think helps any woman keep house a little more easily. I instruct my house-keeper to thoroughly clean one room each day instead of try-ing to clean the whole house at one time. I mean, to go over that room from top to bottom: getting cobwebs from ceiling corners, dusting, vacuuming, polishing the furniture, and so on. If this is done one room at a time, the entire house will have been cleaned by the end of the week. I do the same thing when cleaning out drawers. I love well-organized drawers, so I make it a practice to quickly straighten one out every morn-ing. Doing this on a daily basis will keep the drawers in your house fairly well organized.

Organizing your grocery shopping can also save a tremendous amount of time. Most women have a tendency to shop too often. Some even stop by the store every night after work. But shopping once a week can save time *and* money. First, you save the gasoline used by going back and forth to the market. Second, there's no way in the world you can just "run to the store for a loaf of bread." I have always said that the smartest salesperson who ever lived was the fellow who invented the shopping cart. How many times have you stopped at the grocery for a single item and ended up filling that empty cart? Your shopping time will be more efficient if you will always shop with list in hand. Anytime I use the last of an item, I list it on a memo board I keep in my kitchen. Then, before I go to the grocery, I transfer my list to paper and I stick to it. Clipping coupons is a way of life in this country, and I must admit I also get a kick out of having the cashier hand me back several dollars. But coupon clipping can be time-consuming. I've organized this task by keeping a small clipper and a small alphabetical file. When I find a coupon for a product I use, I file it away alphabetically for my next trip to the grocery. The whole process is streamlined, and I feel good about saving that two or three dollars.

Even a woman with a housekeeper often ends up doing a great deal of cooking. Of course, you may enjoy cooking as I do and look upon it as a form of relaxation, or as a time for the family to gather for a community project. For example, I enjoy preparing a good breakfast, and one favorite item is fresh-baked biscuits. Now, I know that I could pop a commercially prepared biscuit in the microwave, but I like them made from scratch. Measuring flour and cutting in shortening every morning is time-consuming, so I found that I could save time by storing a large batch of dry biscuit mix on a shelf. Each morning, I would simply take one heaping tablespoon for each biscuit, add a little milk, roll it out, and pop it into my toaster oven. By the time they were ready, I had finished cooking the bacon and eggs. The same mix doubles for pancakes, just add a bit more milk and some sugar. The way I fix biscuits is nothing special, it merely illustrates how you can cut corners without sacrificing your family favorites—it just takes a little pre-planning.

All of us must be creative about organizing our meals these days. With so many family members going in so many different directions, it's a challenge to keep nutritious, low-fat meals on the table. More and more Americans are eating in restaurants as the normal course of events. Besides saving food preparation and clean-up time, eating out can be a terrific way to settle a busy, active family around one table at once. But having said all this, I still think we should pay a little more attention to warnings that this trend is introducing dangerously high levels of fat, salt, and sugar into our diets.

One of my favorite examples of organization in the kitchen comes from a top Consultant on the island of Guam. The next time you complain about preparing dinner, think of this lady—she had ten children and a husband who liked the whole family to follow the island custom of sitting down every day to a hot noon meal. While managing this feat, our Consultant was also holding two classes a day and becoming Queen of Sales for her unit. When I met her, I asked, "How in the world do you accomplish it all?"

Then she told me her method. She did not hold classes on Saturday but used that day to supervise her family as they cooked and froze enough meals for an entire week. Then each weekday morning, the children helped her set the table and get breakfast. After those dishes were cleared, they set the table for lunch and went off to school. Before leaving for her nine o'clock class, the Consultant put frozen meals in the oven and set the automatic timer. By eleven-thirty she returned home to find the meal cooking away, and by noon her husband and children were seated around the table. By one-thirty the cycle had repeated itself and she was off for an afternoon class. At four o'clock she was home again to greet her children as they returned from school and to enjoy a light evening supper. That's being organized!

I believe every woman can take a lesson from this example and save a great deal of time around the house. The key is to have a plan and to delegate work to other family members. I told you how my children helped me fill orders, but they also had regular household responsibilities. I really believe that children should have family duties, regardless of a family's financial circumstances. My children had to care for their own room and do various other tasks such as gardening, raking leaves, washing dishes, and taking out the garbage. If you have children, you know that the greatest obstacle to a plan like this is the daily bickering over whose turn it is to do what or how much is enough. I solved this by developing a standardized performance-appraisal system. Now, I didn't know at the time that I was using a standard employee-management technique—it just seemed like common sense. Nevertheless, it worked. I assigned tasks and carefully listed what I considered to be an appropriate standard of excellence for each job. A task was assigned for an entire week, and during that week, I recorded daily progress on a large poster hung in the kitchen. Each day I would rank each job and give the children grades in the form of little stars. A gold star meant that you had done your job up to standard and without being reminded. A silver star meant that you had done it after being told a couple of times, and a red star meant inferior work. At the end of the week, I added up the stars and used a little formula to calculate each child's weekly allowance. Besides being efficient, I believe this system taught them the consequences and rewards associated with work and performance.

I always remember Parkinson's Law when organizing work: "Work expands to fill the time available for it." How true. Remember the Saturday morning you received a surprise call from an out-of-town friend or relative: "Hi, we're on the outskirts of town and will be by in about thirty minutes." Remember how you managed to get your spring housecleaning done in thirty minutes? Or remember when you had three hours to pack for an unexpected trip, when normally you would have spent two days packing? Well, that's Parkinson's Law in action.

I use this principle to my advantage by giving myself time limits for every little task. When I used to do my own laundry, I'd allow myself three minutes to iron a shirt. If I were making beds, I'd allot two minutes per bed. Or I'd see if I could clean the kitchen in ten minutes. I made a game out of it—Beat the Clock! This was good for me, because it reminded me that no matter what I was doing, my time was valuable. Time is much too precious to waste!

11

Plan Your Life the Way You Plan Your Vacation

WHAT'S A VACATION? Maybe you go to the beach for fun and relaxation, or to a new city for adventure and enlightenment. But it takes a lot of effort to pack up supplies for life on the beach. It's an alien environment for most people, and you may have to get used to new things like the sun and the noise and sand in your sheets. Still, you go to all the trouble because it's *fun*. It takes a lot of effort to travel to a new city. You must have a map to get around; you can get confused on one-way streets and hidden expressway ramps. You can spend half a day walking to the top of the Empire State Building or up every monument step in Washington, D.C.—all in all, it's a very hard job. But you do it because it's an *adventure*. Some people walk miles across a strange European city when they'd take a cab for a three-block journey back home. They say they do it because it's a *vacation*, and vacations are for expanding your horizons and learning about new things.

Why can't you approach every day of your professional life with the same enthusiasm and spirit of adventure you devote to the hard job of vacationing? Why can't you expand your horizons, learn about new things, and most of all, have fun?

Well—I think that you can. There are only three prerequisites. First, you have to pick a job that you truly love—something that challenges and fulfills your individual strengths. Second, you have to plan that workday with the same kind of detail you use when planning a vacation. And third, you have to start looking at your career as if you expected to have some excitement and fun.

Picking a job that you love is both simple and difficult. The difficulty comes when you must sit down and decide who you are and what makes you happy. After you've figured that out, finding a job that fits is relatively simple. I'm not a psychologist, so I'm not going to pretend that I know how you should discover your inner self. But I believe a good place to start is by recognizing your real strengths and by recognizing those things that are most important to you. As you know, I'm a great believer in making lists. And when I'm confused or troubled by a decision, I list all the advantages and disadvantages of a specific solution. Somehow, it helps me think more clearly when I can see facts on paper. For instance, I knew from an early age that I wanted to pursue a profession in which I could help people, compete against myself, meet great challenges, and make a reasonable living for my family. At first I thought it might be medicine, but I discovered that those same needs were met first in my sales career and then when I began my own business.

After I had discovered what I wanted from work, I had to have a plan. Have you ever had one of those Saturdays when you got up in the morning and didn't have a single thing planned for the day! You drifted from one thing to another, and by the end of the day you realized you hadn't accomplished a thing. You felt empty, depressed, and frustrated; you'd wasted a day you'd never get a chance to relive. Well, just as you drifted through an entire day, some people drift through a week, a month, a year—and even a lifetime.

Yet those same people may do a great job of planning their vacations. Suppose your husband comes home from work one day and announces, "Honey, I have two weeks' vacation starting August first." Suddenly you have lots of plans.

"Oh, wonderful! Let's see, where shall we go? How are we going to get there? Where shall we stay? What kind of clothes will the children need?"

Every single detail is worked out. You plan that vacation down to the last item. On that first vacation day, you know exactly what you are going to do and as a result, you have a successful trip.

But what happens when you get home? You fall back into the same old routine. You get up in the morning, hurry off to the same old job, come home in the evening with nothing planned, watch television, and go to bed. The next day follows the same pattern. At the end of the week, nothing's changed, and you're right back where you were on Monday. At the end of the month, and at the end of the year, you're just where you were the year before. Without goals, you can waste your entire life, with nothing to show but a feeling of frustration and dissatisfaction.

If you were going to drive to your vacation destination, you wouldn't start without a road map. The same should be true of your life. Without a plan—a road map—you will never get where you want to go. To accomplish anything significant, you must sit down and decide what you want from life. These are your long-term goals. And as with your $35,000 list, getting them on paper makes them more concrete.

Often when people list long-term goals, they seem overwhelming. But as the old Chinese proverb relates, "The longest journey begins with a single step." In other words, to accomplish great things, you must achieve one small goal at a time. New Consultants joining Mary Kay Cosmetics are urged to hold five skin-care classes during their first week in business. It's important to set realistic, short-term goals—goals that you can actually attain—then go on to bigger goals as you gain self-confidence.

At the same time, a good goal is like a strenuous exercise—it makes you stretch. Goals should be slightly out of reach to be of maximum value. When I say, "Shoot for the moon," I don't mean that you should set ridiculous goals. Set goals you can obtain—but stretch yourself. Remember, if you shoot for the moon and miss, you will still be among the beautiful stars.

At a recent sales conference, I talked to a Beauty Consultant who was just so enthusiastic and so excited by what she had heard there that she had decided to go home and shoot for the moon. She wanted to start producing $1,000 a week in retail sales. The only problem was that, at the time, she was producing an average of $400 a week. I suggested that a smaller, more realistic goal—one of $500 per week—might be more appropriate. I reminded her of another old saying, "Inch by inch, it's a cinch; but, by the yard, it's hard." "Don't just look at the $500 figure," I told her, "break it down into *daily* goals. Five hundred dollars a week represents a daily goal of $100. You should book a class for every day. And if you don't reach the $100 goal, come home and begin calling your customers for reorders until you do."

No matter what the final goal, it's very important to set attainable daily goals—then meet them. If you fall behind your goal by $20 one day and $40 the next, you soon feel so far behind that you'll probably just give up.

In another example, a very ambitious young woman approached me for advice about beginning a business. She had some retail experience, and it was her goal to open a national chain of dress shops. She told me all about her plans to open in several large cities, and eventually expanding even into Canada. But not once did she mention how she was going to operate her *first* store.

Finally I said, "Why don't you concentrate on doing a bang-up job on just one dress shop in your hometown? Really learn how to operate a single store; then, when you've achieved that, you can plan to open a second, a third, and so on. In the meantime, trial and error will help you iron out any significant problem. After you have several stores successfully operating in your own city, expand to another city. Later, you can move into a neighboring state. If you proceed in this manner, one step at a time, you will eventually be in charge of your national chain."

I told this young entrepreneur that she should set her sights on short-term, attainable goals. Otherwise, that great big lifetime dream would be overwhelming. It's great to think big—but take care to break that big goal into smaller goals or plateaus that you can achieve by stretching yourself. This chapter seems to contain several old sayings—well, here's another: "You can eat an elephant, one bite at a time."

The world is full of people who are very quick to dream and very slow to act. Often it's because they have failed to break big goals into manageable goals, but more often, it is a fear of failure. Many people are so afraid of failure, that they never try anything. You can only overcome such fear if you are willing to get up and get started. The death of fear is in doing what you fear to do. Yes, you're going to make mistakes along the way, but you'll also be learning. And as I said earlier, *we fail forward to success*. You *will* make mistakes, and sometimes you will be frustrated as you work toward your goals. But for every failure, there's an alternative course of action. You just have to find it. When you come to a roadblock, take a detour. Go in another direction. Don't let a stumbling block stop you. Go over, under, around, or through it, but don't give up. Have confidence in yourself, and you'll find another route. Remember, obstacles either "polish us up" or "wear us down." A diamond was once just a hunk of coal until it was put under pressure and polished to perfection.

In the previous chapter, I spoke about the importance of putting your daily plan on paper—that $35,000 list of your six most important tasks. I believe you can even extend that principle a bit further. I used to take a bar of soap and write my weekly goals on the bathroom mirror! Each week, I set my goals and then put them right up there in front of me for the whole family to see. If my goal was ten skin-care classes during that week, I put it right up there on that mirror. Then as I held each class, I made a hash mark to indicate where I stood. Having that visual reminder really crystallized my thoughts. I found that if I lost a booking, I'd make every attempt to get a new one for that week, because I *expected* myself to hold ten classes. I did the same with other goals. If I wanted to recruit two new people the next week, I wrote it on the mirror.

I found that I looked at the mirror quite often, but I didn't stop there. I also wrote my goals on notecards and attached them to the sun visor in my car, on my refrigerator, and to my desk. I kept them everywhere, to constantly remind myself (and everyone else) of what I wanted to do for the week. Soon, those goals would be so deeply embedded in my subconscious mind that everything I did was naturally geared toward helping me reach them. I just automatically did the right things, because I programmed myself to succeed!

I've had people tell me they wouldn't dream of broadcasting their goals like that—what if they should fail? But I believe it helps to let others know what you intend to do. To illustrate my point, let me tell you about an experience I had when I first began my sales career.

I had been with Stanley Home Products for three weeks, and I wanted to attend the company's annual convention in Dallas. At this point, I was averaging about $7 a party, so I knew I had a lot to learn, and I thought the convention would be a good place to start. The cost of the trip was $12, including the chartered train fare for a round trip from Houston to Dallas and three nights at the Adolphus Hotel. (So you know how long ago that was!) I didn't have $12, so I had to borrow it from a friend who first gave me a sermon about how I *should* be spending the money on shoes for the children instead of running off to some "wicked convention like men go to."

I had only one other dress and no suitcase, so I emptied my Stanley case and packed my things. I didn't know whether or not the $12 included food, so I packed a pound of cheese and a box of crackers, just in case. (To this day, I feel more comfortable if I have cheese and crackers in my room.) Because I had no extra money, all the hotel bellman got for carrying my case was a very sweet thank-you. That didn't go over any better then than it would now.

But the trip was worth it, because those three days changed my life. I watched them crown the top salesperson Queen of Sales and present her with their supreme sales award, a beautiful alligator handbag. With every fiber of my being *I wanted to be standing in that spotlight.* I sat in the back row of seats, because since I was so far down the ladder, that's where I belonged. I had only been with the company three weeks, and my $7 party average was about as low as you could go. The Queen and I were opposite in every way. She was tall, thin, brunette—and successful. I was neither tall nor thin, and I was probably the most unsuccessful person in the room. But I was so impressed with the crown, the alligator bag, and most of all the recognition bestowed upon the Queen that I vowed, on the spot, the next year I would be Queen.

Among the things they told us that day was, "Hitch your wagon to a star." I hitched to that Queen so hard, she must have felt it—even from the back row! Another principle they taught us was to "Get a railroad track to run on." At that time, Stanley didn't have a sales manual or written guide to follow, and I needed a railroad track. So afterward I went up to the Queen of Sales and begged her to put on a Stanley party one night, so that I could learn from her. She agreed (probably because my admiration was so obvious), and at her demonstration I took nineteen pages of notes. That sales demonstration became my railroad track, and those notes became my springboard to success.

The final lesson I learned at that convention was "Tell somebody what you are going to do." I could immediately see that this was very important in setting personal goals. After all, you should broadcast your goals, not keep them a secret. So I thought, "Who do I tell?" I decided that if I was going to tell someone, it might as well be the president of the company. Can you imagine? There were a thousand people at that convention, and among them sat little Mary Kay wearing a hat so awful that my associates laughed about it for ten years. (And the worst of it was that I didn't *know* they were laughing for the first nine!) Nevertheless, I straightened that hat and marched up to the president, Frank Stanley Beveridge, and said, "Next year *I* am going to be the Queen."

He should have laughed—I must have looked ridiculous. And if he'd known that he was talking to the newest salesperson with a $7 Stanley-party average, he probably *would* have laughed. But instead, he took my hand and held it for a moment, looked me squarely in the eye, and said, "You know, somehow I think you will." Those few words literally changed my life.

He probably forgot the incident within five minutes, but his words were inscribed in my memory. I broadcast my goal, and *the* president of the company thought I could do it. After that, I could not let him down.

Throughout the following year, I *failed* forward to success. I took my nineteen pages of notes and memorized them. Although our personalities were very different, I could see that the words of the Queen of Sales were much better than my own. Obviously, she had succeeded where I had failed. So I used *her words,* and my sales immediately jumped from $7 to $28 a party. Her presentation became my railroad track until I could work out my own.

At the end of that year, I really *was* the Queen of Sales. You will remember that the previous year they had given the Queen an alligator bag. Well, such an expensive handbag was far beyond my financial means, so I set my heart on winning it. I even carried a picture of a similar alligator bag and used it to remind myself of my goal. And wouldn't you know they changed the prize and gave me something else! I can't even remember what it was—I just know that it *wasn't* an alligator bag.

Bag or not, I had become Queen of Sales by setting a goal, breaking it down into small realistic tasks, and broadcasting it to the world.

At Mary Kay Cosmetics, we've always believed in spelling out just what one must do to move up the Ladder of Success. This makes it easy for our Consultants to set their own personal goals. One of the things that had always bothered me about other companies was how nobody ever told you what you had to do to advance. You just had to work and wait until someone finally said, "Surprise! You're a manager!" I decided that if someone *knew* what she had to do to be successful—she would do it. *She would have direction.*

If you select a career that meets your personal needs and if you carefully plan the steps you should take to reach your goals, having fun with your work will naturally follow. To me, life is no brief candle—it's a splendid torch that I want to burn brightly before I pass it on to future generations!

12

How to Succeed in a Man's World by Really Trying

IT DOESN'T MATTER if you are married, single, widowed, or divorced—if you are a woman, you walk a unique path in the world of business. This is because that world is still a man's world. The most obvious illustration of this is in the pocketbook. Nearly *half* of the nation's workforce is female. Fifty-three percent of all women over the age of sixteen are working (or are seeking work) outside the home. And yet women earn and average of only 70.6 cents for every dollar earned by men.

I am often asked how I was able to beat these odds and succeed in a man's world. I can only tell you that when I started my own business, I was middle-aged, had varicose veins, and had no time to fool around.

Much of my attitude about myself and the kind of career I could pursue came from an exceptional woman, my mother. She never once told me, "You can't." During my first marriage, I realized my long-awaited dream of attending college, and at that time I wanted to be a doctor. These were the days when other mothers were telling their daughters to shoot for more "realistic goals," but my mother was telling me to go ahead. She had been a nurse, and she realized that nurses were then second-class citizens in the health profession—handmaidens to the doctors. She didn't want that for me, so she said, "Be a doctor."

As I told you, my plans changed, and I made my way in a career that was actually more suited to my strengths and needs. But the confidence instilled by my mother made me believe I could accomplish anything I set my mind to.

I called upon these strengths once again when, against all odds, I began Mary Kay Cosmetics. In reality, I only planted the acorn from which the giant oak has grown. But this growth came about because we were able to meet a career woman's needs in ways that were not being attempted by any other company. We let a woman learn and grow to her fullest capacity—to be anything she was smart enough to be.

I recently heard a very good definition of a woman's needs. From birth to age fourteen, she needs good parents and good health. From fourteen to forty, she needs good looks. From forty to sixty, she needs personality, and from sixty on, she needs cash. I agree with this statement, except that with the way our economy is going, she will probably need cash even sooner.

Today there are more than forty million women in the labor force, and this number will surely rise as we see an escalation in the costs of educating children, utilizing health care, and providing our families with essential goods and services. Today women are better educated than they have ever been. Women outnumber men in the nation's under-graduate colleges, and in graduate school the ratio is almost equal (51 percent men and 49 percent women). As a result, the old-fashioned notion that a woman's career is a two-year interlude between college and marriage has at long last been retired.

In my opinion, many women working outside the home are more interesting, better wives, better parents, better members of the community, and more knowledgeable than ever before in history.

And yet I recently read a report that really dismayed me. It was a survey taken by the National Industrial Conference Board of New York City, an independent, nonprofit research institution.

Founded in 1916 by leading American industrialists, this organization provides objective data on economic trends and practices. The report indicated that while men's salaries have increased to meet rising inflation, women's salaries have remained stagnant. As a result, we are being paid proportionately less than we were in the year 1939. Even after the Equal Pay Act of 1963, the average woman still earns just 62 percent of what her male counterpart earns. Perhaps you can then understand my pride when I tell you that the average earnings of a Mary Kay National Sales Director exceed $100,000. Or my pride when business analysts report that we have more women earning more than $50,000 per year than any other company in the nation. I think you will agree with me that this is truly "man-sized" pay! Even more exciting is the news that these women are also teaching other women how to do exactly the same.

It always troubled me to earn less than my male peers. I knew that a woman had to be twice as good to receive just as much. But as a struggling young career woman, something else troubled me, too. That was when I presented new ideas to an employer and was told, "Oh, Mary Kay, you're thinking just like a woman again!"

At that time, "thinking just like a woman" meant that there was something *wrong* with your thinking. It's hard to believe it now, but at one time, most women actually accepted such an idea. We must understand that women had been second-class citizens and had been brainwashed into believing such nonsense. Women *do* think differently from men, but such differences are in no way inferior to or incompatible with the way a man thinks. The truth is that thinking like a woman can be a tremendous advantage.

Women have a special, intuitive quality that many men do not possess. Let me give you an example. A while back, two men from our administrative staff and I were walking through a hotel lobby. We were on our way to a meeting, and because the hotel was crowded with Mary Kay Consultants, people stopped us every few steps. We passed two women who were talking quietly and who made no effort to speak to us. Suddenly I stopped.

I walked over to them and said, "Is anything wrong? Can we help you?"

Our Seminars had attracted so much attention that we found it necessary to issue identification badges, and it seemed that these women had lost theirs. They were on the verge of tears, and were standing there not knowing what to do. We made the necessary arrangements for duplicate badges and went on to our meeting.

As we were moving out of earshot, one of the men turned to me and said, "That's amazing. How in the world did you know that those women needed help? All we did was simply pass by."

"I really don't know," I answered. "I just knew that something was wrong."

My male companions couldn't get over the fact that I could take a single quick glance toward those women and detect a problem. But I believe that women are often more sensitive to the subtle signals people give out and thus notice things most men never see.

Our Consultants are often very intuitive, too. Many times they'll understand what a person means, even though he or she may say the exact opposite. For instance, suppose a woman has a facial, puts on new cosmetics, looks absolutely terrific, shows great enthusiasm for the products, and then says, "I might buy it some other time." Very often, a Consultant will sense that the woman is not really revealing the complete story. The woman may even say, "On second thought, I don't like this." The way she looks at herself in the mirror, though, tells the Consultant that she really *does* like it. Using the skills of observation and intuition, a good Consultant recognizes the real reason for the hesitation—the woman doesn't believe she can afford the cosmetics. At this point the Consultant can say, "Did I mention that you can hold your own skin-care class and earn whatever products you want?"

More often than not, the woman will immediately seize the opportunity to earn what she couldn't afford to buy *and* to pass her enthusiasm on to others.

One very interesting example of woman's intuition occurred when we opened our first shop in the Exchange Park Mall. You can imagine how desperately I needed Consultants. So much so that I applied the "three-foot rule" to everyone I met. (If they came within three feet of me, I asked them if they wanted to be Consultants!) By opening day, I had recruited nine people.

There was one man among them who seemed to have more enthusiasm and more ideas than everyone else put together. He looked like a real winner. But somehow, on opening day, I found myself standing with him out in the mall and saying, "I'm sorry, but I just don't think you'll do." It certainly wasn't because he was a man. And I truly didn't have a single fact to back up my feelings. But my intuition was telling me that something was wrong.

Remember, this was our very *first* day in business, and my life's savings were on the line. If the business didn't work out, I would lose everything and have to go back to work for somebody else again. My head was saying, "You idiot! This man has a lot on the ball!" But my heart was saying, "You're right, Mary Kay. There's something wrong here."

The man was absolutely furious with me and said, "I'll show you. I'll start my own cosmetics business in competition with you!"

I said, "Well, okay, good luck!"

Six months later, I opened the newspaper to see a front-page story about him. He had been indicted on a felony charge. Had he been a member of our organization, we may have had a "Watergate" long before anybody else!

Intuition is just one of the special qualities God gave women. Another very precious one is femininity. I truly believe He made us feminine for a reason, and we should always strive to maintain our femininity. I definitely believe that women should pursue any career they wish, but I don't think they should totally abandon looking and acting feminine. There's no reason for a successful woman to behave like a man. For example, it really turns me off when I see a woman dangling a cigarette out of her mouth. And I don't think women should reduce themselves to cursing. I've seen women join in with the profanity when they're around men—and some of them are actually better at it than any man. But I believe this is wrong. I recall one meeting at which I was the only woman present, and someone said, "Since you're here, Mary Kay, I guess we will have to clean up our language."

I said, "Gentlemen, I'm happy to be one of you. I will ask or give no quarter; however, if any of you are looking for an excuse to clean up your language, be my guest!"

When a woman behaves like a lady, she sets the stage, and as a result, men will conduct themselves as gentlemen.

If I know that I will be the only woman present (and this still happens quite often), I go out of my way to dress extra attractively that day. (So what if I *am* a great-grandmother?) I find that men respect a woman who retains her femininity, and that they respond more favorably to her if she presents an attractive appearance.

I've also learned that when I'm the only woman present, it's wise to keep my mouth shut until I am certain that I know what I am talking about. I do not use this technique out of fear—I have never been afraid to speak my mind! But I recognize that the men present will perceive my views differently than they would those of another man. I know that when I do speak, they will listen—and I want to be absolutely on target.

Recently I talked to a woman who's been in business many years, and she made a very interesting observation. She believes that men don't expect as much from a career woman as they do from a man. Furthermore, this can be an asset instead of a liability. "A well-groomed saleswoman," she told me, "can often get in to see a male executive who would turn a man away. In fact, he's likely to hold the chair for her!" In other words, men will often give a woman a little extra assistance. And a woman who is smart will take advantage of this small edge.

When I stress dressing in an attractive, feminine way, I *don't* mean wearing sexy clothing. A career woman should always dress in a businesslike manner. I am, for example, adamantly opposed to women wearing slacks on the job. We have made safety concessions in our manufacturing and warehouse areas, but in all other departments within Mary Kay Cosmetics, women employees do not wear slacks. We are in the business of helping women look more feminine and beautiful, so we feel very strongly that our Beauty Consultants should dress accordingly. We suggest they always wear dresses or suits to skin-care classes, and we also emphasize well-groomed hair and nails. After all, can you imagine a woman with her hair up in curlers, wearing jeans, calling herself a Beauty Consultant—and trying to tell other women what they should be doing to look good? Those women would have to think, "What in the world can *she* possibly tell me about looking beautiful?" We want our Consultants to be the kind of women other women will want to emulate. We're selling femininity, so our dress has to be ultra-feminine.

I believe that dressing in an attractive manner is an advantage for any woman—no matter what her profession. It just makes sense to have as much going for you as you can. Not long ago, I witnessed a very good example of my point. I had been contacted by a woman (I'll call her Dr. Smith) who was gathering material for a book on self-made American women. Her credentials were very impressive—she had been in business herself and she held a Ph.D. My son Richard thought the book was a worthwhile idea, so he and I agreed to spend an afternoon with her.

I wanted to look like a chairman of the board for the interview, so on the day she was to fly in from another state, I wore a black silk suit and diamonds. The interview was scheduled to begin at two. About five minutes before two, I stepped outside my office, and spotted a dreadful-looking woman approaching my secretary's desk! She was wearing a pair of slacks, a short-sleeved shirt, and some sneaker-type shoes. She had a masculine haircut, wore no makeup, and really looked as if she should have been out gardening. In fact, her fingernails looked as if she

had been out gardening. I knew she couldn't be one of our people, because that sort of dress and grooming is taboo in our
office.

I called my assistant, Jennifer, aside and said, "For heaven's
sake, get that woman out of here before Dr. Smith arrives."

Jennifer came back in a moment and said, "Mary Kay, that
is Dr. Smith."

I couldn't believe it!

Jennifer brought the woman into my office and we immediately got off to a bad start. Her first question was about our
company image; and of course, I had to repeat something she
already knew—we stress femininity and good grooming. But
as she glanced down at her attire and unkempt hands, it was
clear that we had a difference of opinion.

I was very relieved when Richard walked in. I thought,
"Oh good, the rest of this afternoon is going to go better."

But when he opened the door and glanced at her, he said,
"Excuse me," and started to leave. He was certain that he had
made a mistake in schedule. This *couldn't* be the professional
woman we were expecting.

"Oh, Richard, just a moment, please," I called. He came
back.

"Richard," I said, "may I present Dr. Smith?" His face told
me that he was completely amazed.

Richard spent a total of five minutes with that woman
before he politely excused himself. He could have contributed
immensely to her research, but he was so turned off by her
appearance that he didn't want to give her the time of day. I
think there's a good lesson in the way Richard reacted. He had
lost his respect for her when he saw how carelessly she was
dressed. No matter what you do, or how restricted your time,
you should always make the effort to look your best. After all,
you only get one chance to make a good first impression.

I think it makes sense for a woman to try to have everything going for her. An attractive appearance is something
every woman can achieve—if she really wants to do so!

I love speaking before women's groups and sharing my beliefs about the special challenges and rewards of being a career woman. Often I will relate my list of helpful "don'ts":

> Don't whimper, cry, or pout to win a point;
> Don't be late;
> Don't be afraid to take a stand; and
> Don't ever lose your control or your cool head.

There is absolutely no reason why a woman should not succeed in business. All she needs is:

> Intuitiveness;
> Foresight;
> Product knowledge;
> Market knowledge;
> Guts;
> Lipstick;
> Clear judgment;
> A stubborn streak;
> A computer.

I believe that God gave women special qualities, but because of this, He also requires more of us. Everything a woman touches should be ennobled. We have an obligation to inject into world affairs all those traits which have long been considered female. These include such things as honor, integrity, love, and honesty. I believe it's wrong for women to feel that they must emulate or copy men in order to succeed.

God created the world, and He said, "That's good." Then He created man, and He said, "That's pretty good, but I can do better." So He created woman.

You are God's masterpiece—make the most of it!

13

Getting Your Career Off to a Winning Start

I BELIEVE THAT the *only difference* between successful people and unsuccessful people is extraordinary determination. If you see someone enjoying a career that you would like to pursue, ask yourself, "What has he or she got that I can't have fixed?" In other words, "How can I do it, too?" I believe that any woman can build a successful career if she has determination and the willingness to work at self-improvement. If you aren't happy with yourself, climb back up on God's easel. He's not through with you yet.

Don't forget that although I was a young woman when I first entered my career, I had *retired* before founding Mary Kay Cosmetics. So if you're not satisfied with your status quo, it's never too late. It took God a long time to get me ready for the role that He had for me.

A career is something much more than a job. It implies a level of commitment, responsibility, and involvement that goes far beyond spending your time and drawing your pay. As you mature beyond the idea of a mere job and approach your work as a career, there are many things for you to consider. Not the least of these is the path you will travel to reach your long-term goals. You may want to risk investing money and time in an independent business venture. Or you may want the security of an ever-growing salaried position. In either case, it's essential that you know how to present yourself and your abilities.

Remember, whether you're approaching a prospective employer or seeking financial backing for your own business, it's *your job to sell yourself*. There are a thousand other people competing within any profession, but you can give yourself an edge by thinking about what you have to offer. So many people approach a new career by asking, "What can this do for me?" instead of "What can I do to make myself and my services invaluable? What unmet needs can I fulfill? Sometimes this attitude can mean the difference between success and failure.

Your first task is to honestly evaluate the skills you already possess—to take an inventory of *yourself*. What are your assets? What do you do well? What do you really want to do—not just for the moment, but for an entire career? What kind of a career will bring out your own natural enthusiasm? Put these evaluations down in black and white, because until you actually commit them to writing, you may be fuzzy about those things you can actually do. On paper, your abilities become very clear. Don't forget abstract qualities. For example, you may list traits such as "I'm attractive. I like working with people. I'm outgoing. I'm energetic. I'm determined." Once this task is complete, I'm certain you will discover that you are a *very* special person.

Your list will also identify areas in which you can improve. These may include furthering your education, organizing your family responsibilities, or developing some other personal skill.

Remember that the truly successful career is built upon three requirements. First, you must have the desire to succeed, or as I call it, the "want to" spirit. Second, you must have "know-how." Knowledge is power; it builds enthusiasm and enthusiasm builds success. But neither desire nor knowledge is enough—the third requirement is that you also apply yourself. You can want to succeed with all your heart. You may learn everything there is to know about your career. But unless you are willing to *apply* these skills—in other words, to work hard—all of your efforts will be wasted.

Perhaps you will apply your skills to the development of your own business. Perhaps you will decide to become an entrepreneur. Every entrepreneur I've ever met has been an incurable optimist. My favorite definition of an optimist is that person who when given a barnful of manure runs through it shouting, "I know there's a pony in here somewhere!"

Financial analysts tell us that by the end of this century, the greatest area of economic growth will be in the creation of small independent businesses, such as those developed by Mary Kay Consultants.

One primary reason for such growth is the worldwide trend toward streamlined management systems. More and more companies are consolidating jobs and thus reducing the number of middle-management positions. More than anything else, the explosion of knowledge has contributed to this change. A department head within a large corporation can now plug into his or her computer and retrieve the information once compiled by a dozen clerks. This creates a "squeeze" on a very large pool of talented and experienced individuals. And what can a displaced middle-manager do? Often the answer is to start his or her own small business.

A small business can also be the ideal solution for people currently working in an economically depressed field, people changing careers, or people wishing to enter work with friends or family members. The focus of such a business could be anything from a small manufacturing facility (such as a cottage industry) to a professional service provider (such as a physician or an attorney). Not every entrepreneur plans to develop an international conglomerate—some are simply independent persons who wish to support their families while practicing an art or a trade.

But while the distinctions are many, there are also some similarities. And unfortunately, the greatest is that most of these new businesses will fail. The reasons for failure are as varied as the people involved, but a common problem is undercapitalization. I think it's important to note that while we began Mary Kay Cosmetics with $5,000 capital, it would take much more than that now.

Even so, it obviously takes more than money to succeed. Product and market knowledge are essential, because you really must build a better mousetrap if the world is to beat a path to your door. You must determine which products and services are not being skillfully applied to the marketplace.

Your ability to judge the market and your place in it can be hampered by emotion. In fact, for many people, the only reason for entering business is *emotional*. But simply *wanting* to start a business is not a good enough reason. A woman may love decorating her own home so she thinks, "I want to open an interior-design shop." But she must consider whether or not the community already has enough skilled, well-established decorators.

Before trying to begin a new business, you should carefully analyze your own strengths and weaknesses. For example, what is your level of training or business education? Many women want to enter glamorous professions, such as fashion, even though they have little or no experience in this field. You might consider taking a part-time or temporary job in your chosen field. That way you can gain some real insights into the kinds of skills you will need to bring to your new career.

Women have many talents that they may have never thought of as career opportunities. If you wish to start your own business, begin by asking yourself what you really do well. What makes people say to you, "If you ever decide to go into business, you should take up . . . "? Some of the most successful new businesses were started by women working out of their homes, using their special talents. I know of one woman who had a fruitcake recipe passed down from her great-grandmother. She began her enterprise by selling a few home-made fruitcakes at Christmastime, and it has now grown into a huge industry selling thousands of fruitcakes and employing hundreds of workers. You may know of her company as Mary of Puddin' Hill. As with many successful cottage industries she still maintains those qualities (such as hand mixing) that ensured her original success.

I have witnessed numerous such examples: a woman who developed a large drapery and upholstery company from her work as a neighborhood seamstress, and one who created a successful infants' shop after making baby clothes for her grandchildren. Still another woman began designing maternity clothes after she became pregnant and could not find a suitable wardrobe.

If you decide to become an entrepreneur, you must also be willing to work harder than you would ever work in an ordinary job. A woman who starts her own company, or becomes an independent saleswoman, is her own boss. If she is going to succeed, she has to work for the most exacting boss in the world—herself. I often tell our Consultants, "You must discipline yourself to work as if you had a boss standing over you." This means that you must set aside exact hours to work every single day. Ask yourself, "How many hours *can* I spend on my work?" Once you have made the decision, you must stick to those hours, *no matter what*. Early in my sales career, I decided that at eight-thirty every morning, I would begin work on something that had to do with my job. Then I would spend my day as if I were supervising someone else. For example, when I calculated the value of my time—on straight commission—I recognized that I couldn't afford to stop for coffee breaks half a dozen times a day. You, too, will need to be a strict boss if you are to avoid failure.

But enough talk of failure! You want to know about success, right? While a new business can fail for many reasons, success is usually linked to one vital factor: the ability to satisfy unmet needs. When we began Mary Kay Cosmetics, no other company was actually *teaching* women how to care for their skin. All of the other cosmetics companies were merely selling rouge, lipstick, or new eye colors. So we entered the market ready to fulfill a real need. We knew that we could help a woman understand why she should take care of her skin, and how this could be easily accomplished.

One woman who identified such a need and filled it was Betty Graham. She was a secretary who knew that there had to be a better way to correct typing errors. So she experimented in her kitchen until she came up with the formula for Liquid Paper. Before she died, her company was sold for more than $40 million!

One of my favorite success stories concerns the late Mary Crowley, my longtime friend and owner of Home Interiors & Gifts. Mary and I each had a profound influence on each other's careers. I especially enjoy telling how she founded one of the country's most successful direct-sales organizations.

I met Mary in the early 1940s, when I was with Stanley Home Products. It was a bitterly cold night, when the streets were sheeted with ice and the radio stations were warning people not to leave their homes. But I had a Stanley party scheduled, and I was very conscientious. If I had a party booked I went—ice or not.

Well, Mary Crowley was very conscientious, too—she was the only other person to show up. As the Sunday school teacher of the hostess's children, she felt an obligation to keep her commitment, and so nothing, not even that terrible weather, could stop Mary. I quickly realized there was no point in trying to put on a sales demonstration for her and the hostess, so I decided to just enjoy the cake, coffee, and good company. Both women were lovely people. Mary was an especially exciting personality; she really had charisma.

As we talked, I discovered that she worked as an assistant to the president of the Purse Manufacturing Company. This was before the freeways had been built in Dallas, and getting downtown every day was a real problem. I mentioned to her that I was able to arrange my working day so as to avoid rush-hour traffic, and that seemed to impress her. Like me, she had young children, and the fact that I could be home by four o'clock in the afternoon also interested her.

After we were better acquainted, I asked her how much she earned as an assistant to the president. She looked at me as if it were really none of my business (and it wasn't), and replied, "I make $66 a week." In those days, that was a lot of money.

I said, "Well, I do too—in a bad week." *That* really impressed her. But when I offered her a job as a Stanley dealer, she refused.

I told her, "You would be fantastic in sales, and I think you're wasting your time behind a desk. If you ever change your mind, call me."

I didn't hear from her for more than a month, and then one day she phoned to tell me that her husband had been called up for reserve duty in the National Guard. "I'm going to be home alone for three months," she said. "Do you think I could sell Stanley part-time?"

Usually I had little interest in part-timers, but remembering Mary's wonderful personality, I consented. The first party she observed was a disaster. I made a total of $4. But this didn't discourage her; before long, she had become a Stanley dealer. And she was terrific!

After a few months, she called and told me she would be at the Monday morning sales meeting. She had resigned from her job and was going to sell Stanley full-time. That was the beginning of something wonderful for me, because with her assistance, my unit soared.

Later, when I moved to St. Louis, Mary had done such a fantastic job that Stanley allowed her to take over my Dallas unit. She continued to earn tremendous commissions, until she left to accept the position of sales manager for a fledgling young company, World Gift.

A year later, we were moving back to Texas, and I stopped off for a visit with Mary. She took me to a World Gift show— only this time *she* recruited *me*. I took a World Gift demonstration case, and within a year my unit was doing a major portion of the company's total business.

Meanwhile, Mary left to create Home Interiors & Gifts, her own multimillion-dollar success story.

Mary continued to influence my life for many years, but perhaps the most significant event was when she introduced me to Mel Ash. Mel was in the wholesale gift business and was making a call on Mary's office. As he invited Mary and her husband, Dave, out to dinner, Mel asked, "Do you know anybody else like you?"

Mary answered, "As a matter of fact, I do." Then she picked up the phone and called me. I was a bit reluctant, but I agreed to join them for dinner the next evening. A few minutes before our dinner engagement, Mary called to tell me that "something unexpected" had come up, and that she and Dave couldn't make it! I suspected she was playing Cupid, but I agreed to go. And I never regretted it for a moment.

Isn't it wonderful how, once in a while, someone crosses your path and turns out to have such a dramatic influence upon your life? And to think that if Mary and I had not ventured out on that bitter cold night, we might never have met.

I believe that Mary is a wonderful example of how a woman who uses her talents *can* succeed at anything she sets her mind to. First she was an excellent assistant to the president of her company, then a top salesperson, and later an outstanding sales manager. Eventually—when she had developed the necessary skills and recognized an unmet need—Mary began a small business that grew into a large successful company.

As you begin a new career, remember that whatever you *vividly* imagine, *ardently* desire, *sincerely* believe, and *enthusiastically* act upon must *inevitably* come to pass.

14

Looking Good and Feeling Great

SOMETIMES A WOMAN will come to a Mary Kay skin-care class, literally sit there with her arms folded, and say, "I'm too old. I'm too ugly. And there's nothing you can do about it. I'm hopeless." We try to gently coax and persuade such women with comments such as, "Your face will feel so soft and nice. Please try, I know you'll enjoy it."

If the Consultant is sufficiently tactful, the woman will usually consent to having a facial. Once her skin looks and feels better, she'll agree to try first some Day Radiance foundation, and then a little of the color cosmetics. An hour later, the Consultant will find it difficult to pry the mirror from the woman's hands—because suddenly she *feels pretty*. And it's obvious that she likes the feeling. When a woman feels that she looks good, she simply radiates self-esteem. She goes home with her head held high, and she even seems to walk with more pride. I think the experience is similar to the elation we feel after any great personal victory or accomplishment.

Often the physical change we observe is like a miracle as a woman sits before a mirror, takes one of our palettes, and changes from an ugly duckling into a beautiful swan. The opportunity to witness such physical and emotional transformations is what makes our business so rewarding.

It's no wonder that when economists list depression-proof

industries, cosmetics ranks right up there with beer and cigarettes. During the Great Depression, for example, beer was obviously an inexpensive way to console oneself. And before we knew about the health hazards, people smoked to ease tension. When times are bad, a woman may not be able to afford a new dress, but she *can* still get a lift by buying a new lip color. In fact, buying new cosmetics can often do as much for your spirits as going out for a fancy lunch.

I've known for some time that even in the most extreme cases, cosmetics can be of great benefit to a woman's morale. Take the case of a woman who has been seriously ill. One of the primary indications that she is on her way back is when the medical staff comes in one day and discovers that she has done something about her hair, put on a little lip color, and added a touch of makeup. I personally observed this phenomenon every time I visited my mother in her Houston nursing home. One of her first questions would always be, "Oh, honey, did you bring your beauty case?" Of course, I always had. Then Mother would ask, "Darling, would you fix my face?"

Each time I made Mother up, everyone in the nursing home told her how pretty she looked. And even in her eighties, she really enjoyed that! After making up her face, I would do her hair; she would put on a pretty dress and go out to see her friends. It's hard to explain how these simple steps improved her outlook on life. Mother got such a positive reaction that one day her roommate asked if I could give her a facial as well. So I did, and she received the same compliments.

"Hmmm," I thought, "wouldn't it be wonderful if a Houston Consultant could go to the nursing home one day a week and give facials. It would be strictly a goodwill gesture, and as a side benefit, Mother could entertain six of her friends. It would really be something for these women to look forward to."

At a meeting of the Houston Consultants and Sales Directors, I submitted my idea. I pointed out that because there were fifty-five Consultants present, each could volunteer to take a single week and we would have a program lasting more than a year. Everyone agreed it was a great idea, and that they would love to help these older women feel better about themselves. The Consultants knew they would not make any money from these classes, but it would be a good deed. Because my daughter, Marylyn, was a Sales Director in Houston, I asked her to schedule the first skin-care class for her grandmother. When I told Mother about our plan, she was very excited. It gave her a chance to give something to others, and she immediately invited six women for the following Tuesday.

Marylyn arrived at the appointed hour and gave Mother's friends their facials. They absolutely loved it! But what none of us had anticipated was that the women ordered $156 in merchandise! After that, Mary Kay Consultants scheduled regular skin-care classes at the nursing home. Before long, almost every woman there was using Mary Kay cosmetics, looking better, and *feeling* better.

A few years later, our company was able to participate in a scientifically controlled experiment at the Golden Acres Nursing Home in Dallas, which proved that looking good makes people feel better. My doctor, Herman Kantor, called one evening and asked if he and his wife could stop by my home. When they arrived, he explained that he was on the board of directors of the Golden Acres Nursing Home, and that they wanted to conduct an experiment to determine if or how improving a woman's appearance could improve her mental attitude. Dr. Kantor explained, "We decided that because of the way Mary Kay Consultants conduct skin-care classes and improve a woman's self-image, there is no better company in the world to take part in the research." He then told me that the entire program would be monitored and evaluated by a team of doctors, including a psychiatrist and psychologist.

There were approximately 350 residents in the home at the time, and the researchers felt they needed at least 60 volunteers in order to have an adequate scientific study. At first, it was difficult to interest that many women. They would say, "Honey, you're twenty years too late." We also found that some people would rather sit motionless in front of the television set, or sleep. Many of these women had little zest for life, and we all found it very depressing.

Finally, we did persuade 60 women; we trained the volunteers who would be coming in at seven o'clock each morning to help them with a daily cleansing routine and makeup application. The program commenced.

Two months later, I went by the nursing home to see how things were progressing. It was absolutely amazing! I found women with their makeup on, dressed in their best clothes, and wearing jewelry as if they were going to church that morning. I couldn't get over the change!

In the beginning, the men had not been included in the research, because no one thought a seventy- or eighty-year-old gentleman would be interested in such a thing. But as I talked to the residents, at least half a dozen men came up to me and said, "We demand equal rights!" They wanted to be in the program, too!

At the end of six months, the program was a documented success. A tremendous change had occurred. Women were getting up early in the morning and asking, "Where's my skin-care volunteer?" At the end of the program, the residents invited me to a luncheon in my honor. They had intended the luncheon to express their gratitude, but what truly moved me was looking out at that audience and recognizing such a remarkable transformation. Everyone I saw was dressed up, alert-looking, and bright-eyed. That was all the thanks I needed.

Dr. Kantor's wife had spearheaded the research project, and after the luncheon she said to me, "Mary Kay, there is one person who couldn't join us today, but I think you would like to see her. Would you come upstairs with me?"

She took me to a ward I had seen when I had first toured the home, six months earlier. This was where they placed individuals with serious mental problems. I had vividly remembered one particular woman who had completely lost her ability to reason. She was like a child, and so slight that she sat in a child's high chair. That was where she spent each day, secured, so that she wouldn't fall and hurt herself. She had been sitting with her head down on that high-chair tray, day after day, for three years. In all that time, she had never shown any awareness of the world around her. She had never spoken a word or recognized a living soul. I knew, however, that the doctors had decided to include her in the experiment. As we walked upstairs, Mrs. Kantor explained that each morning the volunteer would have to hold up the woman's head in order to give her a facial or put on makeup. During this experience, the volunteer would speak soothingly to her; then, after she'd finished, put the woman's head back down on the tray. There she would stay until the nurses fed her, bathed her, or put her to bed.

As we approached the woman in the high chair, Mrs. Kantor stopped and said, "This is Mary Kay, the lady who has given you your cosmetics."

With that, the woman actually raised her head and looked up. A faint smile flickered over her face—the first reaction she had shown in three years! As far as I was concerned, that faint flicker of a smile made the whole program worthwhile.

What happened in that nursing home was very dramatic, but every day I see how cosmetics can completely transform a woman and her feelings about herself. I'll never forget one incident that occurred during the early days of our company. We were running ads to recruit Consultants in Sherman,

Texas. We had announced that as a way of introducing our new products, we would give a complimentary facial to any woman wishing to come and meet us. The response was poor, and then at four o'clock radio stations announced that a very bad snowstorm was under way.

"Let's pack up and leave," I said, "or we're going to get snowed in." As we were hurriedly packing, the phone rang. It was a woman who sounded better than anyone I had talked to all day. She said that she lived just a few blocks away, so I told her to come over as quickly as possible.

The Sales Director with me wanted to get back to Dallas before the roads became any more hazardous, and so she was very unhappy with this new development. But I insisted that the woman sounded like a very good lead; then I added, "I hate to leave without having found anyone here."

As we were putting everything out again, there was a knock. I opened the door to the most gargantuan woman I had ever seen. She was at least six feet six inches tall, and was wearing a pair of tight black pants and a black turtleneck sweater. (And believe me, her end did not justify her jeans!) In addition, she was wearing a black snood (one of those old-fashioned crocheted hairnets that women sometimes used to cover up a "hair-don't"). She had on absolutely no makeup at all.

I looked at my Sales Director's raised eyebrows and could just imagine what she was thinking, "The best of the day, hmmm?" There was no doubt that this woman did not fit the picture I had painted.

But we had promised a facial. So while I went to the lobby to check us out, the Sales Director began giving this woman the *fastest* facial in history—complete with makeup. At that time we were still selling wigs, so as a finishing touch, the Director plopped a lovely, long blond wig on the woman's head. This wig had looked gorgeous on the mannequin, but had been at least two inches too large for anyone. But for her—it was perfect.

When I returned, the woman was sitting in front of the mirror with tears in her eyes. I want you to know that you have never seen such a transformation in your life! She actually looked beautiful! Finally, the woman spoke, "This is the first time in my whole life I've ever been pretty."

I knew that she had no money, because earlier on the phone she had told me that her husband had been out of work for some time. She also told me how much she loved him and their two children, and how much she wanted to help him. She took off her wedding ring, her most precious possession, looked up at me and said, "Mary Kay, would you let me go home and let my husband see me looking like this just once? I'll give you my ring as security." Of course, you know I let her wear that wig home.

We drove to Dallas through the snowstorm, but remembering the feeling I had when I saw her joy made it all worthwhile. When we arrived back at the office, Richard told me that was the last time I could ever take chickens, pigs, or rings in exchange for merchandise! But nonetheless, the lesson was clear: a tremendous change comes over a woman when she looks good and knows it. And when she *doesn't* look good, she doesn't *feel good* about herself. Suppose a woman is in the middle of baking a cake and discovers she's out of cinnamon. She's in jeans, her hair is rolled up, her face isn't made up, and she knows she looks terrible. But she must have that cinnamon, so she decides to dash down to the neighborhood grocery to get it. Invariably she'll meet someone she didn't want to see, and it's awfully difficult to hide behind those tomato cans.

But let's say that same woman is on the way home from a wedding, knowing she looks her very best. If she meets someone then, she has an entirely different attitude. She'll radiate confidence. There's no question that a woman who looks prettier on the outside will feel more self-assured.

Some years ago, I was holding a training class in Houston.

One of the Consultants in the class had never had a $100 skin-care class. She had been with the company about three months, and she had been to one training class after another. Yet somehow, success seemed to have eluded her.

In talking to this class, I said, "You must feel confident. Before your skin-care class, do your hair and your nails. And if you don't have a dress that makes you feel like a million dollars, go buy one." (I had no idea of the effect *that* statement would have on her!) "If you have just one dress in your closet that makes you feel terrific, one that wins compliments for you—wear that dress to every class until you can afford to buy a second one."

This woman and her husband had been enduring severe financial difficulties, and she hadn't bought any new clothing for three years. But she left the training class and went directly to buy a new dress. That night she had her first $100 class.

Well! She was so excited! She decided that if a new dress was the answer, she should buy another before her second class. And she did. On the evening of her second class she again sold $100 worth of merchandise. She repeated the procedure for her third class—and had still another $100 class. All in all, she had purchased three new dresses, and had three $100 classes! On the following Monday, she bounced into the sales meeting and announced, "I've found the secret! All you have to do is buy a new dress!"

Of course, that wasn't the secret at all. The secret was that at long last she was confident in her appearance and, as a result, she was able to project more enthusiasm and conviction in her presentation. By the same token, many of our Consultants have what they call a "lucky" suit—one certain suit that always seems to ensure a successful class. It's really a state of mind. But often you will hear, "Every time I wear my red suit, I have a $200 class."

Frequently a woman entering our organization will not know how to dress or present herself. But invariably she will

Mary Kay and National Sales Directors in Bermuda, summer 1993

Mary Kay presents a commemorative plaque to the consultant who purchased the one millionth copy of her autobiography at Seminar 1992.

Receiving the Horatio Alger Award from Dr. Norman Vincent Peale, 1978

Kathy Helou, Queen of Unit Sales, Sapphire Seminar 1993. Kathy was the first Director to achieve Unit retail sales of more than $2 million in one year. She debuted as a National Sales Director in 1994.

Mary Kay and Linda Flagler, Queen of Recruiting, Emerald Seminar 1993

Mary Kay and Judy Caraway, Consultant Queen of Personal Sales, Ruby Seminar 1993

Mary Kay and Wanda Tiet Thai, Queen of Recruiting, Diamond Seminar 1993.

Mary Kay by pink Cadillac

With son Richard Rogers, Awards Night

strive to "fit in" with the women around her. Before long, she will undergo a more substantial change as she blossoms into a confident and successful sales professional. All of us like to fit in with our peers, and so we also find that if a new woman does not value good grooming, she will usually "shape up or ship out." It reminds me of schoolchildren. If everyone else is wearing jeans, the little girl forced to wear a dress will feel uncomfortable and apart from the group. ·

I've mentioned how important it is for a woman to look good, but I think a man cares just as much about his appearance. I am convinced that we may soon see the day when men will once again use makeup. Just glance in a barbershop and count the number of men lined up under the hair dryers. Unfortunately, you'll often see a man with handsome clothes, good-looking shoes, an expensive briefcase, well-groomed hair, manicured nails, *and* skin that needs immediate care! If you look back in history, you will see that there have been many times when men did use makeup and wear wigs. A woman keeps. *her* skin clean and healthy; she uses makeup to accentuate or diminish specific facial features. So why shouldn't a man do the same thing?

Perhaps the only thing currently preventing men from using makeup is the fact that in the recent past such a practice was considered unmanly. But not too long ago a real he-man would not even dream of using deodorant. Fashion and opinions certainly change.

Even so, many people are surprised to learn that we have a successful product line for men. Not long after we began our company, we noticed that many women were reordering basic skin-care sets much sooner than necessary. We were concerned that these customers might be using the products inappropriately, so we would call and say, "Let's review how you are using the Masque or the Night Cream. You shouldn't have used your Basic Set up yet, and perhaps you are overdoing it."

After a few minutes of conversation, a woman would often admit that she had used the products so quickly because her husband or boyfriend was using them too! She would explain that he had seen how great her skin had begun to look, and so behind closed doors, he would give himself a facial. After several such incidents, we decided to introduce our Mr. K line. I felt that many men would feel foolish using something out of a pink jar labeled "Mary Kay," so we designed a masculine package and changed the names to more masculine names. For example, Night Cream became Moisture Balm, and Cleansing Cream became Cleanser. The brown-and-silver Mr. K containers were packaged in a handsome tote bag that easily carried them when traveling. Our current line, called Skin Management products for men, is now specially formulated for men's skin and takes into consideration their specific skin-care needs. Today, the Skin Management line commands approximately 20 percent of the men's skin-care market. Most of these products are purchased by women for their husbands, sons, and boyfriends. But when men become more open about their need for good skin care—we'll be ready!

Looking good makes you feel better. I believe that at Mary Kay Cosmetics, we are in the business of helping women (and men) turn these good feelings into more positive self-images. This, in turn, will allow them to approach life's challenges with confidence and determination. As I have often said, "We're not only in the cosmetics business—we're also in the people business."

15

Happiness Is . . .

WHEN OUR COMPANY became a publicly owned corporation in 1968, I became a millionaire. That poor little girl from the wrong side of the tracks in Houston had finally made it! But I didn't think, "Wow! I'm a millionaire, so *now* I'm happy."

As the song says, "Happiness is different things to different people." I suppose everyone has his or her own definition of happiness, but I'd like to share my formula with you. To me, happiness is, first, having work that you love to do—something you like so much you'd do it even if you weren't paid. Second, happiness is someone to love. And third, it is having something to look forward to.

Contrary to the thoughts of many people, happiness is not guaranteed by money. Very often people who are preoccupied with financial problems think that money will solve everything. And it's true that it's hard to be happy if you don't have enough money to support your family in a comfortable manner. But money is important—only until you have enough of it! By this I mean until you have earned enough to provide good food on the table, adequate clothes, a nice home, and some of those luxuries (such as a television and automobiles) we have all come to feel are necessities.

Perhaps you're thinking, "It's easy for Mary Kay to say that; she doesn't have to worry about money. She's the chairman emeritus of a large company." Yes, that is true—today. But I wasn't always in this position. I know very well from firsthand experience what it's like to live from one commission check to another. I've already told you about the early days of my career, when I had to produce sales or I couldn't pay my rent each month. For many years, I was the sole provider for my three children. And I can assure you, that responsibility is something I will never forget. So if you are someone who is currently struggling to make ends meet—I can truly identify with you.

Although I knew financial hardship, there was only one time in my life when money became a top priority for me. That was when I began saving to buy our first house. I started with nothing, and every week I put a few dollars in my savings account. I still remember how thrilled I was when I finally hit the $100 mark. Then my goal was to add another zero to that figure. When I did, I was on cloud nine. I did all kinds of things to avoid spending money so that my house account could grow. It took years, but I finally reached my goal.

Money, for its own sake, has never been tremendously important to me. I've heard people say that for them, money is a way of keeping score. Often they pass a comfortable income mark and they want to earn more and more in order to measure their achievements. They say it's not the money that excites them, but the idea that they're doing a job worthy of what they are accumulating.

Of course, different things motivate each of us. But I firmly believe that the happiest people are not the ones with the most money but the ones who truly enjoy their work. For me, work is a thrill. Even today, I get up at five every morning and start on my list of the "six most important things I must do today." I love the sense of accomplishment that I feel when that list is completed. I have often said that I enjoy what I do so much that I would work for nothing!

Having work you love to do is an essential part of my happiness formula. I truly feel sorry for all the people in this world who must go each morning to jobs they hate. Stop and think about it for a moment. Out of each twenty-four-hour day, you work eight hours and sleep eight hours. That means that you only have eight hours left for fun! If you are miserable for one-third of your life, it's bound to have a negative effect on the remaining two-thirds.

Some time ago I read an interesting article stating that mental institutions are filled with people who hated what they had done for a living. For each of them, something "snapped" after years of getting up in the morning and forcing themselves to go to jobs they disliked. I find this to be very sad, and a lesson we can all profit from. If you hate those eight hours of work, that emotional state is bound to have long-term negative effects upon your mental health.

Many of the women in our company have written to tell me that their success with Mary Kay Cosmetics has made it possible for their husbands to give up jobs *they* thoroughly disliked and move into more satisfying careers. Often the husbands themselves write to tell me how grateful they are. Many of them felt locked into nonproductive lives until their wives' incomes as Consultants or Directors allowed them to change their own professional goals. When a Consultant tells me that she has earned enough money to give her husband this freedom, her shining face makes it clear that nothing else could ever be more satisfying to her or to the rest of her family.

Of course, the basis of our entire Mary Kay philosophy has always been that it's better to give than to receive. At the very beginning of her career, a Consultant is told, "Your role is not to sell cosmetics. Your role is to go to a skin-care class asking yourself, 'What can I do to send these women home feeling more beautiful on the outside, knowing full well that they'll become more beautiful on the inside as a result?'"

Every Consultant is taught that her role is to give. We have the same emphasis throughout our organization. A Director is told never to look at a Consultant and think, "Gee, this month she can produce X number of dollars in commissions for me." Instead, the Director must think about how she can help the Consultant reach within herself and bring out talents that she never even knew existed. In our business, we get happiness by giving. As someone once said, "Flowers leave their fragrance on the hand which bestows them."

Today, I would say that one of the things that gives me the most happiness is seeing how many of our people love their work with Mary Kay Cosmetics. I often receive letters that say, "I love being a Consultant so much I'd do it for free!" Knowing how many other women share my feelings is truly a great joy for me.

When you enjoy your work to this extent, it's important to have someone to share it with. You can be the most powerful person in the world, but your happiness is somehow incomplete without that special somebody. Think of how many people have found glamorous, high-paying jobs, but who have not found happiness. One good example was the late Marilyn Monroe. On the surface, she had everything. She was beautiful and wealthy, and she had a very exciting career. Yet, at the height of her fame, she took her own life. It is hard to understand how someone in such a position could actually be so miserable. Many of us were shocked when, after her death, people who knew Miss Monroe told of her deep loneliness. How could someone be so lonely when she was always in the limelight and so admired by others? We may have thought, "Surely someone like Marilyn Monroe would have been surrounded by friends and deluged with social invitations." But in truth, her fame and glamour made people feel insecure about themselves. *They* thought that surely *she* would be unapproachable. So instead of finding people who loved her, she found emptiness.

This is why having someone to love and share your time with is a vital part of my definition of happiness. Marilyn Monroe didn't have this element in her life; as a result, she was consumed with destructive thoughts. I think many women, especially widows such as myself, can clearly understand this point. For fourteen years I had Mel to love and to share my joy with. When he died, I suffered a deep and profound loss. But I knew that I couldn't allow myself to be consumed with self-pity. Instead, I put on a happy face as best I could. And just four days later, I resumed my professional schedule. I kept myself so busy that I didn't have time to feel sorry for myself. I believe that when you lose a loved one, you must accept the knowledge that he or she is now in a better place. Our grief, then, is really for ourselves. Life is for the living, and we must carry on with our daily goals and objectives.

We also have to remember that other people may not be feeling sad just because we are. As I approached my first Christmas without Mel, I simply could not find the heart to put up a tree. Then it occurred to me that nearly four hundred Directors were scheduled to visit my home the week before Christmas. Each of those women would be expecting to see my house looking festive. I didn't want to dampen their spirits or the holiday season, so up went the decorations and on went my happy face.

I had this same battle with self-pity the very month in which Mel died. He died on the seventh of July, and on the twenty-second of that month, I was scheduled to entertain Directors coming to an annual conference in Dallas. For fourteen such occasions, Mel had stood beside me as we welcomed the women into our home. He had helped serve cookies and tea; he had always given a short, informal speech to the gathering. This particular July, I felt totally lost. But they never knew it, because I didn't let them know.

With Mel gone, there is still an empty place in my heart. But I am fortunate in having so many other wonderful people to love. And so often, I have the privilege of sharing with the women who work with our company. Not long ago, I received a tear-stained letter from one of our Consultants in Atlanta. The letter began, "Dearest Mary Kay, I'm sitting at my kitchen window this morning watching my little girl run on two good legs. And suddenly it dawned on me that I owe this miracle to you." She went on to explain that her young daughter had been born with a deformed leg, and that the family had been unable to afford the many operations needed to correct the problem. Knowing how cruel children can be, the woman dreaded the thought of her child entering school with that disability.

Then, when the child was about three, the woman attended a Mary Kay skin-care class and realized that *she* could do exactly what she watched the Consultant do. So she became a Beauty Consultant, established a special savings account and for several years saved every penny she made. When she wrote me the letter, the operations had been performed and the child now had two normal legs. This was a woman who knew how to love and share with her family. And I'm so grateful that she also shared with me. Just knowing that one child will lead a normal life is worth all the trials and tribulations of building this company!

The third part of my happiness formula is always having something to look forward to. In my case, this is linked to my first two elements of happiness. I look forward to enjoying my work as much as I always have, and I look forward to being with and sharing with people I love. I think it's vital to always have something at the end of the rainbow. Once you approach your dream, it's important to find still another dream. Haven't you always found it to be true that anticipation is more exciting than the actual realization of your goal? For instance, children are more likely to enjoy anticipating their birthdays than they do the day itself. The same is true of a student anticipating summer vacation or graduation. In our business, we often see what a thrill anticipation can be. When a Director is working to earn the use of her first pink Cadillac, she and her whole unit are excited. But once she realizes her dream, the excitement wears off; and everyone goes about business as usual. I think most people have that same experience with their first house, first fur coat, first diamond ring, and just about any other once-in-a-lifetime thrill. Once the dream is realized, the object that represents it is no longer so important.

I think it's healthy to always have something to reach for, and to replace a realized dream with a new one. By doing this, you stay enthusiastic and excited about life itself. I'm certain this accounts for the high energy level that some people enjoy. I *know* that is what keeps me going strong.

In a beautiful book entitled *The Magic of Believing,* Claude Bristol described his observations as a newspaper reporter. He saw some people die of illness, while others, just as ill, recovered; and he watched football teams win while other teams, just as skilled, lost. After studying this phenomenon all over the world, he wrote, "Gradually I discovered that there is a golden thread that makes life work, and that thread can be named in a single word—*belief!*" Bristol saw the power of belief in action, and he recorded what he saw. People with *belief* do *fantastic things!*

We all need a reason to get up in the morning. We need to keep doing new things that we enjoy and finding new excitement. My own dream is that Mary Kay Cosmetics will someday be the largest and finest skin-care company in the world. This is not a starry-eyed dream, either—we're certainly on target so far.

The truly happy person is one who never finds the end of the rainbow. I've enjoyed so many things during my lifetime—far more than I ever dreamed possible. Still I find it difficult to wait for the sun to come up each new day. This is because I make certain every day that there's something exciting in store. And every single day of my life, I thank God for giving me so much happiness.

16

You Can't Outgive God

I RECENTLY RECEIVED an envelope that held twenty $1 bills. Along with the money there was a note from a Director asking me to autograph each bill so that she could award them to her Consultants. This happens frequently, and I always write the same thing beside my name: "Matthew 25:14–30." That, of course, is the parable of the talents. I really believe that we are meant to use and increase whatever God has given us. The scripture tells us that when we do, we shall be given more. That truth has been dramatically illustrated throughout my life, but I'd like to tell you about one very special example.

Years ago, the pastor of my church asked me to address the congregation about raising funds for a children's learning center. I must admit that my first reaction was a sigh. (Well concealed, I hope.) The fund-raising effort had been going very slowly. Each Sunday, a member of the congregation had made a plea for the special collection, but the results were still discouraging. No matter who spoke, we just couldn't top $600 to $1,000 a week; at that rate, we would not have that building for a long, long time.

With all of this in mind, I felt a little hesitant about accepting the responsibility for an additional Sunday morning speech. Furthermore, I hadn't been involved in the Sunday school program. So I said to the pastor, "But I don't have anything to do with the children's work in our church. Why not ask someone who works in that area?"

"You do believe children should be brought up in the church?"

"Well, of course I do."

"Then say so."

He had me. "When?" I asked.

"How about six weeks from today?"

The pastor was wise. I'm sure he knew that people will agree to anything that's six weeks away. I decided that I couldn't do much worse than anyone else had done, so I agreed to give it a try.

"I'll do it," I said.

The six weeks seemed to fly by rapidly since I was very busy at the office and had some traveling commitments as well. But, in the back of my mind, I was always searching for the right words to include in my plea to the congregation. It bothered me that I hadn't already written my speech, because I usually plan such work far in advance.

Mel and I were in Chicago the week before I was to address the congregation and, once again, I had been unable to find time to simply sit down and write. On the night before my speech, we arrived home well after midnight. I was very worried because the right words still wouldn't come, but I convinced myself that it would be better to get a good night's sleep and plan my speech in the morning.

That morning Mel and I overslept! When I awoke and looked at the clock, it was after ten. I had less than an hour to get my thoughts in order and be at the church! It takes me longer than that to get dressed every morning. *When* was I going to write my speech? I had fully intended to have some quiet time that morning to work up the best presentation I could. And look what had happened! For about five seconds, I thought longingly of just staying home. But that was impossible; I had to keep my promise.

Mel was already racing around getting ready, and so I did the same. I grabbed the first dress I saw in my closet, and as I was slipping it on, I thought, "Lord, fill my mouth with worthwhile words, and stop me when I've said enough." Obviously the speech was going to be in His hands, for I didn't even have time to think!

"You'll have to tell me what to say, Lord," I prayed. And then I stopped dead in the middle of putting on my makeup, because a thought had come to me so clearly and suddenly that I was shocked: "Mary Kay, tell the congregation you will match whatever they give today."

The thought was so vivid that I put down the makeup I was holding and said out loud, "Wait just a minute, Lord! I've got to think this over!" Fortunately, Mel didn't hear me talking away in my dressing room. "He'll think I'm crazy!" I thought. If I even implied that God had actually spoken to me, anybody would be entitled to suggest that I needed a little more rest than I'd been getting. Talking to God is one thing. Many people do that. And I'd heard of people who claim that God speaks to them, but this was the closest I'd ever come!

In the car, I had a moment to think and pray, and I was tempted to tell Mel about my idea. "Don't you dare," I repeated to myself as we rode in silence. I tried to gather my thoughts for my speech; all I could think about was that sentence that had come into my head so very clearly and so unexpectedly: "Mary Kay, tell the congregation you will match whatever they give today."

By the time we got to church, the choir was in place and the service was about to begin. We had to tiptoe down the side aisle to reach our seats. We'd hardly sat down when the pastor called me to the pulpit.

As I walked up, I realized that I still had no idea of what I was going to say. Once again I said silently, "This is in your hands, Lord." Then I found myself talking about the years I taught Sunday school back in Houston. There I worked with four- and five-year-olds and had witnessed the value of teaching the Bible when children were young. I talked about how important it is to teach children the difference between right and wrong. And I remember quoting Proverbs: "Train up a child in the way he should go, and when he is old, he will not depart from it."

Then I heard myself saying, "You know, we've all been talking about this building for quite some time. And each Sunday we've been getting about $600. On a good week, we might even get $1,000. But at this rate, these children are going to have grandchildren before the building is built. We must do something about this.

"You've heard me talk about our company and how we operate on a cash basis. Well, I'll match whatever you give today."

Complete silence. I took a deep breath and went on.

"You know that we operate on a no-credit basis, so I don't want pledges from you today—I want cash or checks!" And then for good measure, I repeated, "Whatever you give today, I'll match."

There, I had done it. I glanced at Mel. Because I had not spoken to him about my idea, and because Mel was retired and might not be able to afford this offer, I really couldn't do it in both our names. Still, I didn't want to hurt his feelings by just doing this in my name. Whatever the amount was—I knew that I was going to have to match it personally.

Mel looked shocked, and so did a few other people. But for the most part, the congregation just sat there. I really could see no reaction at all. As I walked back to my seat, I was already berating myself for an idea that had been a total failure. "Look at you," I thought. "You can sell cosmetics, but you can't sell God's work."

When the pastor finished his sermon, he paused and added, "I had some difficulty keeping your attention this morning. I hope it's because you were thinking of Mary Kay's offer." Then he looked over at me and said, "Mary Kay, I happen to know that a lot of our members make out their checks before coming to church, and so they may not have their checkbooks with them. Would it be all right if we gave them until five this afternoon?"

"That's fine," I said. I was surprised the pastor seemed to think the congregation would respond, but I hoped he was correct. When five o'clock came, I found myself waiting for the telephone to ring. All afternoon I had been wondering how much had been given. But nobody called. I kept checking my watch, and the hours kept passing. With each hour, I became more discouraged. Obviously, the collection was so small that they were embarrassed to tell me about it. The later it got, the worse I felt. Usually I would talk to Mel about my worries, but this time I was just too embarrassed to mention it. I still hadn't heard a thing when it was time for us to go to bed.

It was about ten o'clock the next morning before I finally received a call from the chairman of the building committee.

"I was waiting for you to call last night," I said. "What happened?"

"Well," he said, "we had a meeting about this after church last night, and it got to be quite late."

"Oh. Was it that bad?"

"Oh, no, on the contrary. It was phenomenal."

Phenomenal? $1,000? Maybe more. Maybe $2,000! Or even $5,000? "What do you mean?" I asked him.

"Now, Mary Kay," he said carefully, "before I tell you the figure, I want to tell you what we were debating at our meeting."

"Yes?"

"We spent some time talking about this, and we decided that we do not want to hold you to your offer. I have been charged with the responsibility of making that absolutely clear to you. We know you didn't expect what happened, and we didn't either."

"I made the offer," I said, "and I'll stick to it."

"Now, you don't have to; I want you to know that. We would certainly understand if you didn't."

"How much?" This was beginning to sound more like $5,000! Maybe $10,000. If so, how wonderful! He still hesitated and I thought, "Maybe $20,000?"

Finally he spoke. *"$107,748."*

I was the person who had gone to bed the previous night just praying that they had at least collected $1,000. I have never in my life had such mixed feelings. That $107,748, along with my contribution and what we already had, would be enough to start the building! I had asked God to tell me what to say, and He certainly had. It had succeeded beyond my wildest dreams.

On the other hand, my announcement came back to me very clearly: they had to give cash—and so did I—*today!*

By now the silence on my end of the line was becoming noticeable. "Are you there?" he asked.

"Yes," I sighed. My mind was working furiously. I don't leave that kind of cash in my passbook savings account. As money comes in, I invest it. But those other members came up with it and somehow, I would too. The only solution that occurred to me was to cancel my next appointment and set about arranging a bank loan.

"Now, you don't *have* to," he began again.

"I know, I know. And that's very considerate of you. But I certainly intend to keep my word. In fact, you be sure the building committee knows that it is definitely my pleasure."

I hope I sounded cordial; I'm not sure, because the moment I hung up that phone, I had my head in my hands. That was a lot of cash—about one hundred times more than I had expected to need. "Okay, Lord," I said. "You got me into this. Now you get me out! How *am* I going to get this money?"

Then the phone rang. It was Richard.

(I must backtrack a bit at this point and explain something. Months before this event, Richard had come to me with an investment proposal. A geologist that he knew had developed a seismic technique for finding oil. Richard investigated the procedure and had been very impressed with its potential. As a result, he had encouraged me to invest in two oil wells. I trusted his judgment and told him, "Go ahead." From that day forward, I had never given those wells a thought.)

Richard was elated. "I've never seen anything like it in my life! Everything you put your hand to turns to gold."

"What do you mean?"

"Those oil wells," he said. "Remember? I've just heard that they've come in. Not one, but *both* of them. And both *gushers!* It is unbelievable. Do you know what those wells are worth?"

"Tell me." I'm sure that I'd stopped breathing, because I just had a funny feeling.

"Between the two of them," he said, "your share this month will be more than $100,000."

I can assure you, it was a very humble and grateful woman who took my contribution to the church at noon that day. The money I borrowed from the bank would be paid off by the end of the month with revenues from those oil wells!

This incident reminded me of something I learned as a little girl in Sunday school (incidentally, in a classroom not nearly as nice as those in the new children's building). You never need to be afraid of giving for God—because He will always see to it that you get back a hundredfold. That's what the parable of the talents is all about. The more you give, the more you get. You can't outgive God.

But there is a sequel to my story. After such success, I was approached a few years later and asked to once again head up a major fund-raising drive for the church. This time I decided to take a different tack: I organized other members and we spent six weeks getting the congregation ready for our proposal. One marvelous Sunday morning, we acquired pledges of over *$10 million* for the Christian Learning Center and at another time *$7 million* for the church sanctuary! I've said it before, but now I'll say it even stronger—you can't outgive God!

17

Think Pink

A FEW YEARS AGO, Dick Bartlett, a member of our senior management team, addressed students in the School of Business at Harvard University. Dick always dresses in the professional manner you would expect from a man of his caliber. But upon entering the classroom he was absolutely delighted to see almost every student wearing the color pink. In the years since 1963, all of us at Mary Kay Cosmetics have gained a "pink reputation." In fact, it sometimes seems to us that everyone who "thinks pink" also "thinks Mary Kay." And we love it!

Therefore, people are surprised when I tell them that at the time we began our company, *pink was not my favorite color!* The decision to select the color for our packaging and promotional materials was based upon pure logic. In 1963, almost every home in America had a white bathroom. Then, as now, people usually had their countertops filled with cans and jars of deodorants, hair sprays, perfumes, and cosmetics. Most of their labels were designed in bright bold colors, which I found offensive. I wanted containers that would be so attractive that women would want to leave them out on display. We considered many colors and ultimately decided that a soft, delicate pink would look best with those white-tile bathrooms.

As our company became well known, *everyone* expected me to love pink, sit in a pink office, live in a pink house, and always wear pink clothing. And I will admit to you now that for many years I resisted "pink pressure." It's true that I can be a little stubborn when people tell me I must do something, but I honestly felt more comfortable when surrounded by yellows and blues. I loved conservative black suits; and people often told me that dramatic colors, such as red and blue, were flattering to my eyes and complexion. What woman doesn't like to wear the colors people say she looks good in?

But the color pink continued its hold on me—becoming more and more associated with good feelings, success, and pleasant memories. One day I got the idea of rewarding our top Sales Director with a pink Cadillac. I wanted a Cadillac, because it was the top of the line. I wanted pink because it was "our color," and because it got the attention our top producers deserved. There's no question that people do take notice when a pink Cadillac pulls up to an intersection. When I drive mine, everyone notices, and somehow I receive special courtesy from other drivers. (Our Directors have observed this same phenomenon.) If I am waiting at an intersection to pull into traffic, someone will always graciously motion for me to go through.

Automobiles have become such a hit that they are the core of our awards program. We even created two achievement levels that precede our Cadillac accomplishment—a pink Pontiac Grand Prix, which Directors may earn, and a red Grand Am, available for Directors and top-performing Consultants.

Actually, we give General Motors such a large annual order that they now officially call our color "Mary Kay Pink." How could I resist such a wonderful tribute?

In addition, many, many thoughtful people have remembered me with pink gifts. It seems as though any time a Consultant or Director sees anything pink, she thinks of me! As a result I am always receiving the loveliest pink presents, and we display dozens of these items in large curio cabinets throughout my office and reception area, and in my home. I love each and every one because they all represent the love and success we have been able to share with so many people.

Manufacturers who know we buy hundreds of thousands of awards and promotional items also remember me. Almost daily I will receive samples such as pink pencils, pink stationery, pink paper clips, and so on. You'd be surprised what can be made in pink these days. Sometimes these items are very clever. For instance, we once used a pink calculator as an award in a contest. I even received, of all things, a little pink trampoline for indoor exercising, and some enterprising furrier has offered me a pink mink!

After a while, pink seems to have a very pleasant effect upon people. In fact, a group of California psychologists studied this observation and concluded that the color pink helps calm overexcited and violent people. They found that when unruly prisoners were put into pink cells, most became quiet within minutes!

I don't know exactly how it happened—whether it was the tranquilizing effect studied by the psychologists, or the simple fact that I now associate pink with love—but the truth is that I've come to love pink, too. After all, "if you can't lick 'em, join 'em."

This was dramatically illustrated when I decided to build a new house. During the planning stages, some of my closest advisers came to me and carefully said, "Mary Kay, since your new house will be seen by so many Consultants and Directors, we think it would be nice to carry out our corporate image—and paint the stucco pink."

I really shocked them when I said, "That's a great idea; let's do it!"

The house was built and, I must admit, it was very grand with twenty-eight-foot-high ceilings; a Grecian pool; crystal chandeliers from Venice; a large, paneled reception room with a marble fireplace; a bathroom that was an exact duplicate of one owned by my late friend Liberace; a yellow-and-gold dining room; an open foyer with a winding staircase; and plenty of room for all my guests.

I lived in the pink house for six years and spent much of my time in a relatively small suite that contained my bedroom, dressing room, and an office/library.

18

Applause, Applause

WHEN WAS THE LAST TIME someone gave you a round of applause? At your college graduation? After a remark you made at a church committee meeting? Can you remember how good it felt? Then magnify that feeling a thousand times and imagine yourself standing center stage in the Dallas Convention Center. Behind you are several enormous video screens, each the size of something you'd see in a theater, and each projecting your picture and your name. You are surrounded by a set that rises several stories and is covered in lights and decorations worthy of Broadway. Cameras roll and flashbulbs flicker as thousands of people rise and applaud you. That's what it's like to be recognized at a Mary Kay Seminar, and we call the phenomenon "The Power of the Stage." Professional saleswomen cross that stage for a few seconds and come off trembling with excitement and enthusiasm. From that moment until the next year's Seminar, each will fight to once again earn such applause. That's because every single one of us thrives on recognition.

The annual Seminar is the most important event in the Mary Kay year. This is the time at which individual Consultants and Directors come together to share and acknowledge accomplishment. And we're not talking about a simple "company convention." Seminar is a multimillion-dollar extravaganza that has been called an Academy Awards, Miss America Pageant, and Broadway opening all rolled into one. Seminar has dazzling awards, competition, drama, and entertainment. It is a three-day spectacular—Mary Kay–style.

We go to all this expense and effort because we have learned one very important lesson: the desire for recognition is a powerful motivator. If you give somebody a forty-cent item in a $1 box with $100 worth of recognition, that's a thousand times more effective than giving a $100 item in the same box with forty cents worth of recognition!

Throughout Seminar our National Sales Directors and top sales leaders conduct education sessions in that they address every topic that could help a Consultant build her own independent and profitable business. But without a doubt, the highlight of Seminar is Awards Night. No expense is spared as we strive for elaborate staging and glamour worthy of a Cecil B. DeMille production. The event culminates as our top performers are rewarded with the fabulous prizes that have made Mary Kay Cosmetics synonymous with luxury and glamour: diamond rings, pink Cadillacs, and dream vacations.

Each Awards Night has a theme that expresses a company philosophy or a motivational idea. For example, in one past Seminar the theme was "Dreams Come True." In this particular event, production experts spent months orchestrating and staging a fairy-tale background, complete with a four-story castle, music, knights and their ladies, thousands of twinkling white lights, and musical adaptations from the score of *Camelot*. Even the most blasé person found it impossible to keep from being caught up in the enthusiasm that filled the arena that night. And that's how we want the audience to feel—positively transported to a brighter day and a bigger dream!

Seminar is the ultimate expression of a very simple concept—*praise people to success!* Let people know that you appreciate them and their performance, and they'll respond by doing even better. Applause and the recognition it represents are among the world's most powerful forces.

Everyone loves praise. One of the most important steps I ever took was when I began imagining that every single person I met had a sign around his or her neck that read, "Make Me Feel Important." Whether it's figurative or literal—absolutely everyone responds to applause. I believe that if you had the choice of two gifts for your child—$1 million on one side of the scale and the ability to think positively on the other—the greater gift would be the gift of confidence. And you only give confidence with praise and applause.

Every once in a while I will run into someone outside our organization who will begin to scoff about all our awards and symbols. It may even begin with a silly comment, like "I don't need all those gimmicks to make me do a good job." Or they might ask, "Don't you think those women are foolish to work so hard for just a little ribbon or pin?" But these people have obviously not looked at the world around them.

I heard a cute little story that illustrates how much praise matters to people. It seems a mother and her teenage daughter were having a discussion about the girl's boyfriend. "What does he like about you?" the mother asked.

"Oh, he thinks I'm beautiful and sweet and have a wonderful personality."

"That's nice. And what do you like about him?"

"The fact that he thinks I'm beautiful and sweet and have a wonderful personality!"

But I think when it comes to needing applause, grownups aren't that different from children. Did you ever notice how football players get a star for their helmets every time they make a key play? Well, I don't suppose that's really much different from the gold stars children get for good performance in school. Everybody responds to praise, from a small child to a great big 250-pound macho linebacker! And what about the medals and ribbons on the chest of a professional soldier? People have always been willing to risk injury, and even death, for symbols of recognition.

Praise certainly did a great deal for me when I was a small girl. My mother praised me for everything I did, and I grew to like that recognition and to want more of it. I liked being praised for selling the most tickets and receiving an award for being the best typist in my class. I enjoyed being in the limelight on the debating team. And I loved being applauded at extemporaneous speaking contests.

Seminar is our ultimate recognition, but we practice our philosophy of praising to success many thousands of times a day. And we start the very first moment we meet and encourage a prospective Consultant. When a woman first considers a career with Mary Kay Cosmetics, it's very common for her to say, "Oh, actually, I don't think I could ever sell." What she's really saying is, "I don't have enough self-confidence." I have seen women join our company who didn't have enough confidence to order a pizza over the telephone. I don't think some of them could have even led in silent prayer! But we encourage them by praising even the smallest achievement. We applaud each little success one after another—and the first thing you know, they actually become successful. *We praise them to success.*

One Consultant who came for our new Director development program was so shy she couldn't even say, "Good morning." When I entered the room and said, "Good morning," she just ducked her head. Later, I learned that she had joined the company so that she could someday stand in front of a group of six people and say, "My name is Rubye Lee." That is what I call being self-conscious!

One of the staff members asked me what I thought about her, and I replied, "You know, I don't think that girl is going to make it. I've never met anyone so shy." Little did I know that one year later this same woman would be standing onstage at

Seminar holding thousands of people in the palm of her hand. She delivered a speech so powerful she received a standing ovation. She's absolutely tremendous, and today has risen to the rank of National Sales Director! All she ever needed was someone to bolster her confidence.

Let me give you another example of "praising people to success." It happened many years ago, when we were still at 1220 Majesty Drive. I was in my office one morning, and since our quarters were rather small, I couldn't help overhearing National Sales Director Emeritus Helen McVoy as she talked to a Consultant, just outside my door.

"You had a $35 class?" she exclaimed. "That's wonderful!"

Well, even in those days a $35 class wasn't wonderful. I couldn't imagine who she was talking to, and why she might have said such a thing. So I opened my door to peek out, and Helen saw me.

"Oh, Mary Kay," she said, "may I present my new recruit? Last night she had a $35 class!" Helen paused and added with enthusiasm, "The first two classes she didn't sell anything—but last night. . . !"

Without that praise and encouragement, it's entirely possible that Helen's new Consultant might never have held her fourth class. Helen was praising her to success. Underlining a person's confidence by praising each small success has enabled many people to achieve more than they ever thought possible. It was John D. Rockefeller who said, "I will pay more for the ability to deal with people than for any other commodity under the sun—sugar or wheat or flour!" I'm sure that Helen McVoy's innate ability to work with people is the reason she was the number-one National Sales Director in Mary Kay for seventeen years.

I've already told you how much I wanted to win the Miss Dallas contest held by Stanley Home Products. Why did I work so hard? It certainly wasn't for a ribbon with "Miss Dallas" on it. I worked for the recognition. Since then, I've seen many other women work just as hard for a ribbon as they would have for an expensive gift or a cash prize. You see, it doesn't matter what the prize might be. Even if we are awarding a food processor and a woman already has a new Cuisinart, she will work and work to win. It's the recognition that she needs.

We've found that a woman first entering her career thrives on the praise we give her. No homemaker ever has anyone in her family exclaim, "Oh what a beautiful, clean floor!" "What nice, clean diapers! Aren't they white and fluffy!" And most office workers rarely hear, "It's wonderful how your reports are always free from spelling errors." Even women who do volunteer work may never be recognized for all that they contribute. When any of these women come to us, they suddenly learn how much fun it is to receive recognition and money for their work.

I think most women are willing to work hard for even a tiny bit of recognition. That's why we award a ribbon for a Consultant's first $150 skin-care class, another ribbon for her first $200 class, and so on. Recently a Director wrote to tell me that some of her people had won every single sales ribbon we have. "Where do I go from here?" she asked. I wrote back telling her to start praising those women toward recruiting, and then to help them get on the road toward becoming Directors themselves. Our Directors understand the importance of recognition. Many of them, for instance, give a Consultant a small star for each person she recruits. By the time a Consultant comes to Dallas for our new Director development program, it's not uncommon for her to have fifteen or twenty little gold-colored stars on her jacket. By giving her those, her Director is giving her a visible sign of her achievement. Those stars say, "Look at me—I'm an achiever!"

As important as recognition is, exciting prizes are also important as symbols of recognition. I'll never forget one of the first sales contests I ever won. I worked very hard to win the top sales award; and when I got it, would you believe that it was a *flounder light?* I didn't even know what it *was.* I found out later that it's something you use when you put on those long hip boots and wade out into the water to gig fish! I was proud of winning—but I can't imagine anything I might have wanted less.

I kept that flounder light around for years just to remind myself, if I ever got into the position of giving awards, not to ever give a woman a flounder light! I would try instead to choose prizes that would excite and thrill the recipient. I thought that the best prizes were things a woman wanted but probably wouldn't buy for herself. So in our company, we eliminated most "practical" gifts. A woman will usually think about her family before she considers herself. If you put a washing machine on one side of a scale and a diamond ring on the other, most women would select the practical item. That's how we came to award prizes such as pink Cadillacs and diamond jewelry.

We award countless diamond rings. Except for an engagement ring, most women never receive diamonds. And so in our company, in just a matter of a few years a star performer could have a diamond for each finger.

Anything can be a symbol for recognition. At Mary Kay Cosmetics, one very successful item has been clothing. For example, after a Consultant has recruited three new Consultants, she may wear a special red jacket. And Directors and National Sales Directors earn the privilege of wearing designer suits specific to their levels of accomplishment. (New suits are selected yearly.) Thus, you can look into a crowd of ten thousand Mary Kay Directors and Consultants and immediately recognize our top performers by their clothing. Obviously this tradition is modeled after the uniform distinctions observed in the military. (After all—rank has its privileges!)

Our methods of recognition are not limited to prizes. We also recognize our outstanding people in our monthly *Applause* magazine. People love seeing their names in print, so we list our star salespersons for each month. We also include the names of our top recruiters and new Directors. Every issue is full of photographs of women who have reached some significant milestone in our organization.

About seven thousand Sales Directors also send out a monthly newsletter so they can praise the members of their own units. In many cases, this means recognizing people who didn't make the news in *Applause* magazine but who had significant accomplishments nonetheless. Our corporate office produces a weekly publication for the Directors called *Directors Memo*. And *Memo* often reprints original or especially inspiring stories first seen in the local newsletters. Everyone aspires to be quoted in the *Directors Memo*, so this too has become a form of recognition.

I believe that public recognition is the finest form of praise. Newsletters are one very effective way of giving this recognition, and another is the weekly unit meeting. All our Directors hold these meetings, and they offer an excellent opportunity to praise individuals for their achievements. Being praised in front of your peers is more gratifying than being praised in private. The enthusiastic applause and the presentation of ribbons and other awards adds an aura of excitement. This sort of recognition does wonders for a person's self-esteem.

Giving praise where it is due has become a working philosophy in every aspect of our work at Mary Kay Cosmetics. The praise begins at the first skin-care class a woman attends—when we tell her how she looks after her facial. Then, when she expresses an interest in becoming a Consultant, we encourage her by telling her that she too can do it. Perhaps the time she needs praise most is after she has given her first class. Even though the Consultant may have made some drastic mistakes, a wise recruiter will avoid criticism. Especially in the beginning, the Consultant needs praise for everything she did *right*.

I don't think anyone responds positively to criticism. Suppose a woman spends $100 for a new dress and the first time she wears it, someone says, "For goodness' sake, where did you get that terrible dress?" You can be assured that she will never wear it again. I find that if you must criticize, it's best to sandwich it between two thick layers of praise. For instance, when a Director goes to a Consultant's skin-care class, she may take two pages of notes. But on one page, she should write down all of the *good* things she observed. After the class the Consultant will invariably say, "Tell me what I did wrong." (They all say that.) Instead, the Director should say, "Let's talk about what you did right." And then she must encourage the Consultant by praising her strong points. When she does give the necessary criticism, she carefully sandwiches it in between all the praise. Only then will it be gratefully accepted and acted upon.

Insincerity has a tendency to backfire, so I think it's very important to be honest when you give this praise. I must say that when I was a young saleswoman, I learned this lesson the hard way.

I always made a practice of complimenting my hostess on something I really liked about her house. But at one particular party, I was very rushed and didn't have time to really look around. As I was setting up my demonstration, I noticed a painting of a hummingbird on an orchid, and I said, "What a beautiful painting!"

The hostess said, "Oh, I'm so glad you like it. I painted it."

I couldn't think of anything else to say, so I complimented her again on it. It was obvious I left the impression that I really liked the painting.

Two weeks later, I went back to deliver her purchase. It was almost Christmas, and I desperately needed that money for my children's Christmas gifts. The woman gave me a warm welcome, and then she said, "You know, Mary Kay, I've been thinking about how much you liked my painting. And I'm going to give it to you for my order."

Of course, there was nothing I could do but thank her. And I don't have to tell you what kind of Christmas we had that year. But I learned an invaluable lesson: *never* give insincere praise. (I also learned to say "No, thank you" when someone wanted to trade instead of pay.)

Giving praise is an integral part of our business. Every Consultant learns very early to praise the people she works with. And soon, giving praise becomes second nature. Her habit of praising others has a ripple effect, and soon enriches the lives of everyone she knows.

It was Emerson who said, "The only real gift is a portion of thyself." And we give of ourselves when we give encouragement and honest praise. In the long run, we are the ones who gain, for it is true that all we send into the lives of others comes back into our own.

19

That Personal Touch

MANY YEARS AGO, I stood in line for three hours so I could shake hands with the vice-president of sales for the company I worked with. We had never met, and to me it was a very special occasion. When I finally inched my way up to actually meet him, he did take my hand and say hello—but all the while, he was looking over my shoulder to see how many people were behind me. Even today, I am hurt by the memory of that incident. Then and there I decided, "If I ever get to be the one people come to shake hands with, I'm going to put all my attention on the person in front of me—even if it means I never finish the line."

As things turned out, people have stood in line to shake my hand; and I have always tried my best to make every single person feel important. People have asked, "How do you do it? Aren't you exhausted?" Of course I can become physically tired, but I continue because I know how it feels to be brushed off by someone who's important to you. And whether you're standing in a reception line or talking to your child after school, it's always important to focus all your attention on the person in front of you. If you can love that person, that's all the better. But you must never treat anyone in a way you wouldn't like to be treated yourself.

It's just amazing how important some personal attention

can be to people. It makes a bigger difference than you might think. For example, let me tell you about the time, many years ago, when I decided to buy a new car. They had just come out with two-toned exteriors, and I had my heart set on a black-and-white Ford. Because it's always been my policy to pay cash, I had waited until I had saved up the total price. It was my birthday, and I planned to give myself that beautiful car as a very special present. So, with the money in my purse, I walked into the dealer's showroom.

The salesman had apparently seen me getting out of my old, beat-up car and assumed that I couldn't afford a new model. In any case, he didn't give me the time of day. He completely ignored me.

Well, I was determined to buy that car. I asked to speak to the manager, but he was out to lunch. And because I didn't want to wait around the showroom for an hour with that rude salesman, I decided to take a walk.

Just across the street, there was a Mercury dealer; since I had some time to kill, I decided to walk through his showroom. There was a yellow Mercury on the floor, and it cost quite a bit more than the Ford. But this time the salesman was very courteous and interested in me, and soon he found out that it was my birthday. He excused himself for a minute, and when he came back, we talked for a while longer. The next thing I knew, he was wishing me a happy birthday and placing a dozen red roses in my arms. And that's how I came to buy a yellow Mercury instead of a black-and-white Ford.

I've always believed in the importance of the personal touch. Almost every month new Directors attend sessions in Dallas. And every month, I try to include time on my schedule to meet them.

The incoming Directors love to have their pictures taken with me; and so even though it's sometimes overwhelming, I willingly pose as long as I'm asked. I've stood for hours while photographs were taken of me with every single person present. I've been advised that it would go faster if I just passed them through quickly and didn't talk to anyone. But if I did such a thing, I think the women would feel hurt. I know that this is important to them, so I always have something to say to each person.

Those photographs can also become an important sales tool for the new Directors. For example, Consultants use a flip chart at skin-care classes, and included in our company materials is a picture of me. Often the Consultant will say, "And this is Mary Kay, our chairman emeritus—and a great-grandmother!" The women at the class may yawn and say, "Oh, sure. And that picture was probably taken when she was fourteen years old!" But if she can whip out a photograph and say, "Last month this picture was taken of Mary Kay and me," all of a sudden there's interest and everyone wants to see it. I'm told this causes a lot of excitement, because the women are always interested in current snapshots. It's more personal.

Now that our company has grown so large, the personal touch seems even more important. This is because people don't quite believe that I'm a real person. Very often women will come up to me at Mary Kay functions and say, "I just can't believe it. You're real. And you're just like they said you were."

I think a personal word is so important to everyone I meet. Invariably someone will say to me, "Mary Kay, do you remember when I met you in . . . ? I was just a new Consultant then, and you told me I'd be here someday." Well, I have to confess that I don't always remember every such comment. But when I hear these remarks, I know how much it means to people when I stop and say a few personal words.

Every now and then, the personal touch makes a believer out of someone who thinks I'm more myth than reality. Recently a man called long distance four times and insisted on speaking to me. I was in a meeting, and Jennifer kept telling him that I wasn't available and offering to help. Finally, he told her his reason for calling. "Look," he said, "my wife has become a Consultant and wants to place a large order. But I'm telling her not to do it until I can check out what this company is all about. I want to speak to Mary Kay!"

When I got out of my meeting, I found his name and a note from Jennifer on top of my phone messages. So I called him.

"Well, I've already looked up your company," he began, "and I found that you're doing millions in sales. Actually, I'm amazed that you returned my call. I never really expected to hear from you."

It turned out that he also owned a business, and was very impressed by our personal touch. The last thing he said to me was, "Mary Kay, you made a believer out of me by returning my call."

I was glad to hear that, because he had obviously been giving his wife a hard time, and now he was going to be more supportive of her career.

As I stressed in Chapter 9, it's so important for our company to help Consultants win the support of their families. When a woman comes to our corporate offices for New Director Development, we write a letter to her family and explain how beneficial this will be to her career and thank them for sharing her with us this week. We mail the letter on the Monday she arrives in Dallas so that it reaches her home just about the time the sink is full of dishes and everyone is getting a little uptight about having to do everything without her. I think these are important letters, and I sign each one personally.

As you might have guessed by now, we've been sending out Christmas, birthday, and anniversary cards to every single one of our people since we started this company. We send cards to hundreds of thousands of individuals, and we make certain that every card is mailed on the right day. I personally design the cards, and each card has a message in my handwriting. Some of my favorites are "A wonderful birthday to a wonderful person" and "Precious things are very few—that's why there must be just *one* of *you!*"

At the end of her first year with the company, we also send each Consultant an anniversary certificate. On each of her next three anniversaries, she receives another certificate, and on the fifth year, she receives a lovely pin with the number five.

Each of our several thousand Directors also receives a small Christmas and birthday gift. One year, we sent the Directors a "Ms. Bear" for Christmas. This was something Mel had given me for a Thursday gift. You pulled its string and it said things like, "You're wonderful. . . . You're headed for the top," or "I love you. You are terrific. You can do anything."

I also demand that every letter addressed to me receives a reply. I feel that anyone who cares enough to write deserves an answer. Of course, as the volume of my mail has grown, it's become impossible for me to handle everything myself. So we've developed a system for analyzing and answering letters in a specific manner.

There are many things, of course, that I handle myself. One is sympathy cards. I send perhaps a dozen handwritten notes a day to those of our people who have just lost a loved one. And I also send personal notes to those who are seriously ill. There are a few pieces of poetry that have been meaningful to me in times of sorrow or concern, and I will include a copy in each note. People seem to be very touched by that personal note and poem. When I can, I sometimes make phone calls to extend my condolences or get-well wishes. Sometimes I just call to say that we all love her. A call like that is such a little thing, but it always seems to do wonders in lifting a person's spirits.

We've worked hard at keeping a family atmosphere in our organization, regardless of our size. Nobody is addressed as Mr., Mrs., or Ms. here. Richard is called Richard by everybody, and I'm called Mary Kay. If people call me Mrs. Ash, I think they either don't know me or they're unhappy with me. We don't have titles on the doors, either. And unless there's a conference going on, our office doors are always open. As you can imagine, people will often walk right into the office and interrupt you if you keep the door open. But we feel it's important for everyone to know that they can see us regarding important issues.

You don't find many closed doors in our company, and you also won't find executive bathrooms or executive dining rooms. We have a pretty cafeteria, which I've been told looks more like a country club than a company lunchroom. And it's not just for executives—it's for everyone.

As our company continues to grow, I'm sometimes embarrassed by meeting someone on the elevator who I don't know. If I can tell by the papers he or she is carrying that this person works for the company, I will say, "Hi, I don't think I've met you. I'm Mary Kay." When I recognized how this sometimes flusters people, I decided to participate in our monthly new employee orientation program. These are people who have just joined us, and so they always come in to the meeting very formal and straight-faced. I tell a few anecdotes, talk about the company, and, before long, they relax and begin to smile. I think these meetings help them see me more as a friend than as chairman emeritus.

Occasionally we have had executives join us who couldn't adjust to our family atmosphere. This can happen when they've worked for another company with a more hierarchical system. One executive, in particular, not only kept his door closed but refused to talk to visiting Consultants and Directors. At times, he was downright rude to them. That's just the way things had been done in his former company. (Hard to believe, isn't it?) Finally, I had to say to him, "The only reason you have your job is because of those Consultants and Directors. As far as we're concerned, they're the most important people in the world. Don't you agree that you should feel that way about them too?" He did see that his attitude was wrong, and began to roll out the red carpet when any Consultant or Director approached him. He became much happier at his work and, needless to say, so did everyone else.

Unfortunately, some companies do not have the same respect for their employees. One of our employees related a sad experience with his former employer. His wife had gone into labor in the middle of the night, and when he took her to the hospital they found that the baby was in the breech position. This can be a very difficult situation, and for two days, there was a possibility she wasn't going to live. It was touch and go, so he stayed by her bedside and waited. With all that going on, he forgot to call his office—which was as it should have been. She was the only thing on his mind.

When he returned to work, he didn't have a job, because he hadn't called in. Even after he explained what had happened, they just said, "Well, if you don't think any more of your job than that, you're fired."

This man applied for a position with us because he had heard that we do value the family. He knew that we place the family above the company, and if the same thing had happened with one of our employees, we would have been proud of what he did. When he talked about what happened to him, he would say, "Mary Kay would have sent pink flowers instead of a pink slip." That is our reputation, and I think it pays off. Today, we have a waiting list of people who want to work for us. And the morale of our employees is just wonderful!

In our company, everyone values the personal touch. We believe in courtesy. I remember once a man came in and sat down in our reception area without asking for anyone. Finally, the receptionist asked him, "Is there something I can do for you, sir?"

"Nothing," he replied. "I just came in here to recharge my batteries. I call on companies all day long, and so many people are so sarcastic and nasty, and they bark at me, 'What do you want?' But when I come here, everybody is so happy and smiling, it's like coming into the sunshine. It makes me feel good just to visit this company." I think that's the nicest compliment we could ever receive.

We've had out-of-towners tell us that when they ask to be taken to Mary Kay Cosmetics, their cab drivers treat them like VIPs. "To Mary Kay Cosmetics, I sure will," the driver often replies. "That's the nicest company in town. When I go there to pick up a passenger, they're the only ones who ask me to come in and sit down when I have to wait on a fare. Other companies chase me out."

I believe in the personal touch, because it makes every human being feel appreciated. As someone once said, "The oil of appreciation makes the wheels of progress turn." In our company, we do things that aren't normally done in the business world, but I believe that personal touch has helped to build this company.

Recently a man wrote to me, "Mary Kay, the company is growing so fast, I'm worried that there may soon be a day when that personal touch is gone."

I wrote back and explained to him that I worried about that when we had 1,000 people. Then I worried about it when we had 5,000 and 10,000 and 20,000; I'm still worrying about it now, with more than 325,000 people in our organization! I also told him that I'll *always* be concerned about the personal touch—and do everything in my power to see that we never lose it. Richard feels this way, too, and it gives me great comfort to know that, through him, this important philosophy will continue.

20

The Proof of the Pudding . . .

MARY KAY CONSULTANTS come from every imaginable background and represent every religion; we attract young women, women in midlife, and grandmothers. They live in large cities and rural towns across the United States and in more than twenty countries on every continent. I wish I could tell you about every one of them, because each has a very special story.

With all their differences, they share a common bond—a spirit of living and giving that I believe is unique in the business world. When I began this company, I seemed to stand alone in my belief that a business could be predicated on the Golden Rule. Now, the Mary Kay family has shown that women can work and prosper in that spirit while achieving great personal success.

For some of our women, success may mean earning enough money to send their children to college or buying larger homes. Others set far higher financial goals. However they may define success, Mary Kay women agree that their faith and their families come before their careers. They live the Mary Kay philosophy—God first, family second, career third.

Throughout this book, I have told you about many of the Consultants and Directors who have reached both professional and personal goals. I believe their stories illustrate the real success of Mary Kay Cosmetics. The most valuable assets of our company cannot be found on our balance sheets, for our most important assets are our people. No matter how much profit a company makes, if it doesn't enrich the lives of its people, that company has failed. Our true wealth is measured by the thousands of women who have found our company to be the way to live richer, fuller lives for themselves and their families. In my opinion, that's the *proof of the pudding*.

If you've read thus far about my life, I know you will agree that mine truly is a rags-to-riches story. I did pull myself up by the bootstraps to build a great company. And I am indeed proud of my life and my legacy.

But I am only one person.

Today, in the Mary Kay world, there are thousands of women who have achieved great things in their lives thanks to this career. If you want to read the stories of our top people, I strongly urge that you get a copy of a book we publish called *Room at the Top*. It is here you will find the personal stories of the National Sales Directors, the pinnacle of success at Mary Kay Cosmetics. We call their personal profiles "I" stories.

Reading these "I" stories is truly motivational, and I know for every woman out there, there is an "I" story in the book to which she can relate. It points out the fact that women can rise to the top of Mary Kay Cosmetics from virtually any position, and you'll read in *Room at the Top* how our National Sales Directors have done just that. I must say the stories of their lives make fascinating reading.

You'll read about one of our National Sales Directors who had never written a check before her Mary Kay career and now she earns a lot more than the President of the United States. Another National lived in subsidized housing. One escaped from Communist Cuba. Another couldn't stand the thought of her best friend driving a pink Cadillac!

For many couples, the wife's success in Mary Kay allowed the husband to leave a career he hated. There's one husband who was an economist. His dream was to open a hair salon! There's another who was an engineer who later became a minister, and so on.

There are inspiring stories of single mothers who were trying hard to support their families in traditional "female" jobs such as secretaries, nurses, and teachers before they joined Mary Kay.

One very successful National was a single mother working the graveyard shift on the assembly line at a shotgun shell plant prior to finding us. Another left a promising career in television.

National Sales Directors are former models, Junior League volunteers, women with advanced degrees, and women who never went to college. One of these women baked key-lime pies to supplement her family's income. Another co-founded one of the most successful charitable organizations in Texas.

Whether they overcame devastating illness, or were stymied by glass ceilings in their chosen professions, I think you'll agree that each story has a Cinderella-like quality.

Room at the Top is the tastiest proof of the pudding I could ever offer you because it proves that the theory is correct. That Mary Kay does work in the lives of all kinds of women—every age, every background, every race, color, and creed. These women are absolutely the examples I had in mind for women back in 1963.

Reading their stories is most uplifting. I am so proud of all the beautiful, capable women who have made my dream come true. Not only are Mary Kay women the most loyal and dedicated women in the world, they *define* determination and purpose. They believe that if they work hard enough—and if they give enough of themselves—that they will be successful personally and professionally. They find their lives enriched—with motivated family, close friends, stellar accomplishments, and financial security. And most of all they understand, as I do, how very gratifying it is to be able to help other women achieve their dreams too.

Now that you've heard a few of our success stories, I'm sure you can understand why I love my Consultants and Directors. I'm so proud of all the beautiful, capable women who have made my dream come true. Their success is, indeed, proof of the pudding. As somebody once said, we're a "company that's known for the people we keep." And we think we keep the very best. Mary Kay women are the most loyal and dedicated people in the world. They *define* determination and purpose. They believe that if they work hard enough—if they give enough of themselves—that they will be successful, personally and professionally. And at Mary Kay Cosmetics, they find their lives enriched with friends, accomplishments, and financial security.

21

Leaving a Legacy

ALTHOUGH MARY KAY COSMETICS was created as the dream of one woman, it has long since achieved an independent existence. And because our company is grounded in a solid foundation of specific values and principles, its continuance no longer depends upon any single person.

Business analysts often say to me, "Mary Kay Cosmetics to this point has been a business phenomenon. Certainly everything has gone well for this company. *But what's going to happen when you're no longer here?"*

I explain to them that perhaps there once was a time when the company depended upon me for its existence. The success of just about any new business hinges on the daily presence of one or two key individuals. But we've come a long way since 1963. Our sales force now consists of hundreds of thousands of skilled sales professionals, and they are supported by an experienced management team. We stopped being a one- or two-person company years ago. We would have never realized our present strength if we had not.

Mary Kay Cosmetics isn't the only company that has been identified with one individual. In fact, the founders of many American businesses have been people with very high profiles. During the early days of the Ford Motor Company, there were many people who believed it could not survive without

Henry Ford. But it did. Another example is Du Pont Chemical. This company was controlled by one family for 150 years; there was great concern when, at long last, an outsider became the chief executive officer. But today, Du Pont is one of the largest chemical companies in the world. *Well-managed* businesses will survive any change at the top. If a business can't go forward and prosper without its founder, then I'd say that the founder failed to do his or her job in developing a strong professional management team.

I believe our greatest strength at Mary Kay is our people. As I said earlier, we're not only in the cosmetics business—we're in the people business. And, as a people-oriented company, our primary goal is to offer women career opportunities. In turn, these women fulfill the needs of still other women by teaching them good skin care. In other words, our whole reason for existence is to give people the opportunity to enrich their lives. We also follow that principle inside the company, as we encourage every employee to grow toward his or her full potential.

Without all those wonderful people, there would be no Mary Kay Cosmetics. Of course, it's important to realize that every company has a natural turnover of people as time goes by—this is simply the nature of human existence. But a company remains strong because of its *philosophy*. A company with a strong, basic philosophy can survive anything—even a major change in its products. For example, Du Pont was one of the country's major suppliers of gunpowder from the War of 1812 until World War I. Rockwell International, the large aerospace company, was at one time the manufacturer of parking and taxi meters. And American Express started out as the pony express! All of those companies have successfully adapted to change and as a result are still going strong.

People change and even products change. But over the course of time it's the strength of a company's philosophy that will determine whether or not it endures. The Mary Kay philosophy rests upon three simple and beautiful ideas.

The first and most important is the Golden Rule. We teach our people to treat others as they themselves would like to be treated. Sometimes we call this our "Go-Give Spirit," and we accord special recognition to those individuals who show that spirit in outstanding ways. It's a spirit of sharing and caring for the other person. Many outsiders believe it just can't work, but we *know* that it does work! Our people cheerfully give of their time and experience without thought of what they might receive in return.

The second cornerstone of our philosophy is our belief in the right priorities: God first, family second, and career third. I know many corporate chiefs who think we have our list upside down. But we feel that a person cannot do a professional job if his or her personal life is in conflict. We're perfectly satisfied to be in third place.

Our third cornerstone is our belief in the beautiful potential inside each and every human being. We believe that with lots of praise and encouragement, everyone can be successful. So many women have come to us lacking self-confidence. "Well, I'll try," they say. "I might—if I can." We teach them to throw those thoughts away and replace them with "I can. I will. I must!" Over the years, we've found that positive encouragement and sincere praise work wonders. Everyone *can* be great! The seeds of greatness are planted within us all, and God expects each of us to reach deep within ourselves and bring them into fruition. The countless success stories within our company are proof of this truth.

The continued success of our company depends on these three philosophical beliefs—not upon me. For that reason, I've made certain that everyone in our organization knows how strongly we feel about these concepts. Every management decision is based on our philosophy. Every new Consultant is recruited on the basis of these beliefs and taught to live by them. When a Consultant climbs our Ladder of Success and comes to Dallas for new Director development, I once again reinforce our philosophy with her and her class.

We have had thousands of women who have gone through our programs; in a very real sense, each of them is the safekeeper of the Mary Kay spirit and philosophy. Each Director is the one I'm counting on to uphold our standards by reflecting our commitment to honesty and integrity.

It took God a long time to get me ready for the job He had for me. All my years of experience, trial and error, hard work, and disappointment were necessary before I could be guided to form this company.

We are fortunate to have my son Richard as the Chairman of the Board of Mary Kay Cosmetics. Richard has made me so very proud and won the hearts of our people with his business acumen.

Whatever the reason, someday I will no longer be here. When that day comes, I know our National Sales Directors will carry on magnificently in my place. Every one of them began as a Beauty Consultant and climbed the Ladder of Success right to the top. Our Consultants and Directors know that, so the Nationals will continue to serve as wonderful role models. I used to refer to these women as "the Mary Kays of the future"— but today they already are me. They carry the torch of our philosophy and standards. Therefore, I know that whatever the future may bring, my philosophy will be perpetuated.

Years ago, I worried about what might happen to the company if I were no longer involved. I felt a deep responsibility to the thousands and thousands of people associated with Mary Kay Cosmetics. The company had come so far so quickly that I wanted to be certain it could grow and prosper without me. It had helped so many beautiful women that I wanted to know that those golden opportunities would always be there. I was possessed with the desire to leave a legacy.

I know now that my legacy is assured. The company has my name, but it also has a life of its own. And its life's blood is the philosophy that many thousands of women have made a part of their lives. They *embody* that philosophy of sharing and giving—and as such, it will always live on.

Epilogue

As you perhaps know, my autobiography was written in 1981 and then revised in 1986 to include our "happenings" in those five years. Now, as I write this, it is 1994 and we have enjoyed eight consecutive years of record growth! So much has happened even since that first revision! In 1991 we hit the billion-dollar mark in retail sales for the very first time in our history, and then we did it again in 1992 and 1993.

More than 325,000 Mary Kay Beauty Consultants and Directors serve customers in twenty-three countries worldwide today. All of them are independent business people operating their own Mary Kay businesses—in essence, PRESIDENTS of their own companies.

More than eighty women have attained the position of National Sales Director and our current nationals have average incomes from their Mary Kay careers well into six figures annually. Another seven thousand women are currently Mary Kay Directors. Hundreds of these women make more than $50,000 a year from their Mary Kay careers and many others make more than $100,000 a year. It is estimated that more women have earned over $1 million from their Mary Kay careers than any other company in the world. This makes me very proud.

* * *

There are many other things about this company of which I am proud. For example:

Some 20 million consumers purchase approximately 120 million Mary Kay products each year. Most are manufactured at the company's Dallas plant, ensuring that everything meets our exacting quality standards. Products are then shipped to the company's five regional distribution centers so that Beauty Consultants and their customers receive their products when they need them.

In 1993 Mary Kay Cosmetics had wholesale sales of more than $735 million, which equates to well over $1 billion in sales at the retail level. In 1992 the company qualified for inclusion on the 1993 *Fortune* 500 list, and in 1993, Mary Kay Cosmetics again made the list, advancing fifty-seven spots on the 1994 *Fortune* 500 list.

Mary Kay is the largest direct seller of skin-care products in the United States and is among the three largest United States skin-care companies in dollar volume. As of 1994 we have about 8 percent of the United States skin-care market and 5 percent of glamour products.

Our Mary Kay line includes more than two hundred products in nine categories: basic skin care, skin supplements, glamour, nail care, hair care, body care, sun protection, fragrances, and men's skin care.

Since 1989 Mary Kay has not engaged in animal testing—the Company neither conducts nor causes testing of its products or ingredients on laboratory animals. The Company is an active participant in programs to develop alternative testing methods.

Our company has been widely recognized by such organizations as the United States Environmental Protection Agency for efforts to preserve the environment through such steps as using recycled packaging materials and eliminating unnecessary packaging.

Our annual convention, which we call Seminar, is the largest continuously held convention in Dallas. In July 1993, we drew a total of more than thirty-six thousand Beauty Consultants and Directors for four consecutive three-day sessions. The Seminar tradition is now being continued worldwide. Mary Kay Consultants and Directors around the world have their own Seminars—since I can't attend all of them, I always videotape special greetings.

The most famous of our many recognition programs in Mary Kay is the career car program. Today there are seven thousand cars on the road with a value of more than $100 million. In addition to the renowned pink Cadillac, our car program includes the Pontiac Grand Prix and Pontiac Grand Am. Consultants and Directors earn the use of one of these cars through outstanding sales and recruiting. And, we are now offering cars in many of our international operations. Mary Kay Germany awards a pink Mercedes and Taiwan sales-force members receive a top-of-the-line pink Toyota.

We currently operate in Argentina, Australia, Bermuda, Brunei, Canada, Chile, Dominican Republic, Germany, Guatemala, Japan, Malaysia, Mexico, New Zealand, Norway, Russia, Singapore, Spain, Sweden, Taiwan, Thailand, the United Kingdom, Uruguay, and, of course, the United States.

Mary Kay was included in the original 1984 edition of *The 100 Best Companies to Work for in America* and was one of only fifty-five companies to repeat in the second edition in 1993. We were also listed as one of the ten best companies for women to work for. We were the only direct seller, the only cosmetics company, and one of only thirty-seven *Fortune* 500 companies on the 100 Best list. It pleases me to no end that during this so-called recessionary period, we have continued hiring and had no layoffs.

Mary Who?

It occurs to me that no one ever asks "Mary Who?" anymore. I probably couldn't appear on "To Tell The Truth" as I did in 1980, because most people in America today know who I am. My dream of helping women achieve equality in the business world has become a reality. As a 1978 recipient of the Horatio Alger Distinguished American Citizen Award, I attend the Association's induction ceremony each year in Washington, D.C. It was my pleasure in 1992 to present, along with poet Maya Angelou, the award to Oprah Winfrey. Each year for almost fifty years the ceremonies have honored ten Distinguished Americans. I note that, of the nearly five hundred people who have achieved this prestigious honor, only nineteen are women and only five of those are living and still active. I keep hoping that more women will rise through the ranks of business to achieve this honor.

Now as I write this epilogue to my life story, I truly believe that everything good that has happened to us has been as an outgrowth, an affirmation, of those original principles and philosophies that have guided us from the very beginning. Our company has never wavered from the principles on which it was based: the Golden Rule (do unto others as you would have them do unto you) and our philosophy of God first, family second, and career third. Mary Kay women appreciate the fact that they have time for their faith, their families, and a career. They understand the importance of finding time for those things that are dearest to their hearts.

My fervent prayer is that we never lose sight of our beginnings. These days, as we bask in the present success of our company, we continue to be amazed by all the attention. The Golden Rule, in my opinion, is a way of living, and I'm glad that corporate America is beginning to see that it's also a viable way of doing business. When I read that we are a very large player in one of the three "growth industries" projected for the

1990s, I feel it is a personal confirmation that "thinking like a woman" has brought us to this wonderful place in our history.

By the way, *Thinking Like a Woman* is also the title of a documentary about my life. The story is produced by Martin Jurow, who also produced *Breakfast at Tiffany's* and *Terms of Endearment. Thinking Like a Woman* is factually based, a departure from the way Hollywood often portrays people's lives. However, I say that with the tip of my hat to another Hollywood producer, Norman Lear, who was able to portray a Mary Kay Consultant fairly accurately in his acclaimed film, *Fried Green Tomatoes.*

The Original Purpose of the Book

Speaking of all this attention, would you believe that my original purpose in writing my life story was to lend credibility to our business? At that time in history, our industry and our people sometimes had an image problem. Now, more than a million copies and several best-seller lists later, the book has done much more than it originally was intended to do. We were for real and on the up-and-up then just as we are now.

I am thankful that our industry, direct selling, has become highly respected, and I like to think that we have played a large part in that. On three occasions, I have been honored by our industry. In 1989 I was the first recipient of the National Sales Hall of Fame Award, and that year I also received the Circle of Honor Award from the Direct Selling Education Foundation. In 1992 the Foundation again honored me with the Living Legend Award.

Behind every "living legend" there is a solid foundation. To my way of thinking, it is our twenty-two hundred employees who have served in that role. These are the people whose corporate excellence earned us that distinction as one of the "100 best companies to work for in America." I am very proud of them.

The Dream Continues

Despite all of the success that we have achieved, I see our dream and our work as far from complete.

These past seven years we have doubled the size of our sales force and more than doubled our retail sales. I believe that my dream has changed many thousands of women's lives for the better, and yet I know that there are so many more lives out there waiting for the touch of our hand. There is indeed "room at the top" for many, many more women.

When this book was originally published we had three Mary Kay millionaires. By 1985 the number had risen to fifteen. By 1994 seventy-four had achieved millionaire status. These are National Sales Directors who have earned more than a million dollars in commissions during their careers. It is also significant that twenty-seven of those National Sales Directors have attained *multi*millionaire status, proving my theory that women can indeed do anything in this world they want to do, if they want to do it badly enough and if they are willing to pay the price. The number-one National Sales Director, Shirley Hutton, of Minneapolis, Minnesota, earned an incredible $827,432.45 in 1993.

The earnings potential is unbelievable, but just as significant is the wide diversity among the people who have helped bring us to our success today. The most amazing thing of all is that every single one of these women began at ground zero with the same showcase.

Often we are asked to describe the "typical" Mary Kay Consultant, but this is a description that we cannot provide because it defies categorization. The Mary Kay opportunity attracts women with advanced degrees—Ph.Ds, physicians, lawyers—yet we also have women who were able to leave the welfare rolls and even hopeless poverty because of the Mary Kay opportunity. There are military officers (a war heroine among them) and former nannies. Here's an interesting turnabout. One nanny was brought to this country by an IBM executive to work in her home. That former nanny is now a Mary Kay Senior Director! The former IBM executive is now a member of her unit! Several former journalists have been so impressed with our story, when they became acquainted with it, they made a career change.

Many college students put themselves through school with their Mary Kay incomes, yet we also have a great-great-grandmother in her eighties who is a Director and still very active in the Company.

Mary Kay leaders come from the Harvard School of Business and financial centers like Wall Street. Junior Leaguers and junior-high teachers, opera stars and soap opera stars find this career appealing. One National Football League coach uses our techniques to motivate his football players (his wife is a Director). The chairman of a major retailing chain tells me my book *Mary Kay on People Management* is mandatory reading for all of his store managers. At least a dozen business schools across the nation use the *Mary Kay on People Management* book in their classes, and I've lost count of the number of family members of Mary Kay Directors who have chosen our company for their master's thesis.

Families are indeed very important to us. One of my proudest moments as Chairman Emeritus of this Company came in 1992 when we honored our mother/daughter Director teams at a luncheon with more than 130 in attendance. This event held a special place in my heart since my own daughter, the late Marylyn Rogers Theard, was one of our original Directors.

I feel it is a great compliment to this Company that mothers have found a career they like so much they want their daughters to also pursue it—and, of course, vice versa. I can think of no finer honor. This year we expect to have our first mother/daughter National Sales Director team! Another cause for celebration!

And this is a Company that knows a lot about celebrations. Our grandest celebration is Seminar! You can only imagine the logistics that go into hosting that many people. Hotels and convention facilities are booked years in advance.

Our Awards Night extravaganza during Seminar has become a model for companies around the world. Last year, some thirty-seven hundred of our independent saleswomen were honored with onstage recognition at our Awards Nights—something very uniquely Mary Kay. Year after year, I am constantly amazed at the finesse with which our wonderful staff carries out these special and memorable events.

Speaking of amazing, I guess that's the only word to describe our manufacturing facility in Dallas. Those 120 million products are manufactured each year by people whose quality standards make us all proud. I am told that a typical ten-hour shift, for example, can produce 48,500 jars of cleansing cream! And I still remember how that original chemist turned our formulas over to his son to produce because our business would be too small for him.

Our success has been driven by our wonderful products. It's hard to believe, looking at the five basics that we began with, that today we have products to meet the needs of virtually every woman of every skin type, and even Skin Management products for men. Brand loyalty is at an all-time high.

That same loyalty is seen as we take our dream to every corner of the globe. Women of many nationalities are discovering how to achieve success in Mary Kay and how to make their careers and our products a part of their lives.

It's very interesting to me to note that as we reach out to women throughout the world, every hour of every day someone somewhere is holding a Mary Kay skin-care class.

Sometimes I pinch myself to be sure that this is all real—just like I did when we traveled through the streets of what was once East Germany just sixteen days after the Iron Curtain came down. Driving through the newly opened city in itself was an emotional event, but it doesn't hold a candle to my feelings as I sat onstage in Unified Germany later that evening and honored our first eighteen East German Consultants. One of those Consultants, newly freed from the reign of Communist terror and now for the first time embracing a career of her very own, was moved to take the microphone as she crossed the stage. Her words, spoken breathlessly in broken English, are forever etched in my mind. With tears streaming down her face, she said, "First we get freedom—and now we get Mary Kay!"

Those who know me are not surprised that I am still a member of the Five O'Clock Club, since most of the time I can hardly wait for the sun to rise to get started on my day. Someone once said that we began the "economic liberation" of women in 1963. As I see it, our liberation of women is far from complete. To me it's a good day if just *one more woman* discovers how great she really is and how much potential she really has. America is the land of opportunity—but Mary Kay Cosmetics is the opportunity of the land. Perhaps we really did tap the vein of what women really wanted in the 1960s, but that has only increased in the 1970s and 1980s—and now in the 1990s it has positively exploded.

Three hundred twenty-five thousand Beauty Consultants—and I truly believe our work is just beginning. I am so grateful that God has allowed me to live to see this tremendous success. In the early 1960s God gave me the responsibility of helping women to see that not only could they be feminine but that they could be successful at the same time. I think women have long since learned that femininity is worth keeping. That you do not have to emulate a man in order to be successful.

Just Another Word for Working Harder!

In 1987 I assumed the title of Chairman Emeritus. Today, I can tell you that Emeritus is just another word for working harder! If I trailblazed in the area of economic liberation for women, I've also forged right ahead in the area of remaining active, doing the things that I love to do the most. I've often said, "Find a job you like to do so much you would do it for free—and someone will pay you well for doing it."

I have been rewarded many times over. And yet I still feel challenged to contribute to our continued success.

How active am I? That's the question a journalist asked me recently. On that particular day I was making final decisions on the trim for our next year's Director suit. We custom design these suits each year for our Directors and National Sales Directors, and I must tell you proudly that we have won the National Career Apparel Award for nine consecutive years. After years of winning every annual award, Mary Kay Cosmetics received the "Image of the Decade" award for the 1980s. We have tried very hard to keep our women looking fashionable and well dressed. To this day I am very active in the designing and selection of those suits. In fact, once we have the final sample, I wear the suit for a few months just to make sure that it will perform to the level we expect.

Can you imagine trying to please, fit, and accommodate the needs of seven thousand women in one suit and be very exacting about it? I am of the opinion that we could teach the fashion industry a thing or two about what businesswomen want and need from their clothes. We are operating a real-live fashion laboratory here!

Now back to my typical day. I viewed a tape that had aired earlier on CBS news about the success of our "custom publishing" venture, the quarterly *Beauty* magazine, which we founded with the publishers of *Woman's Day* magazine. Our Product Marketing people brought by a stunning new packaging design that will be introduced later this year. And yes, I have tried all two hundred of our products as they were introduced. At lunch, I took one of our nine National Sales Directors Emeritus on a tour of the Mary Kay Museum and along the way signed autographs for some of the people who were touring our headquarters that day. The number of people who tour exceeds twenty thousand a year. By the way, the Mary Kay Museum at Corporate Headquarters in Dallas is a three-thousand-square-foot tribute to the fact that, as my son Richard says, "She keeps everything."

When the museum opened in 1993, CNN and everybody else who covered the opening made much of the fact that I had even saved our original check ledger (just like the one you use every day). As a matter of fact, I still have the turkey roaster in which I cooked our very first Seminar meal!

My afternoon agenda at the office includes answering just a fraction of the eighteen hundred letters a week that come addressed to me personally. Eight members of our support staff assist me in this effort. We try to answer every letter. I telephoned an employee, a single mother trying so hard to be strong in the face of a devastating illness. We cried together. As large as we have grown, I will never be able to detach myself from the everyday lives of our people, for we really are a family.

I sat in on a brainstorming session for the twenty-fifth anniversary of our Cadillac program. In 1969 we awarded the use of pink Cadillacs to five Directors and now more than seven thousand women drive either Mary Kay pink Cadillacs or other career cars. Imagine that!

Back to my day. There was a baby shower for one of our employees, and then I worked on my "six most important things" list for tomorrow. Because I have a fetish about starting each day with a clean desk, I take home whatever is left when I leave in the afternoon and do it at night or early in the morning of the next day so that when I arrive at the office, everything is finished from the day before. This particular evening, I took home a stack of things that people had asked me to autograph and a two-inch-thick copy of a marketing study that we had commissioned.

Finally, I began collecting my thoughts as a keynote speaker for a Distinguished Women Leaders Lecture Series. I am asked to make a great many speeches, but I try very hard to limit the number, because I feel that my first responsibility as a motivational speaker is to our own Consultants and Directors. People are constantly asking me my secret as a speaker, and it's simple. Our people place a good deal of trust in the things I say, and they know I really do care what happens to them. Through thirty years I have found that thoughtfully chosen words can have powerful positive effects on people's lives and on their careers.

Actually I have enjoyed extemporaneous speaking since the fifth grade. I still remember my fifth-grade teacher's name, Lela B. Scott. It was she who got me on the road to learning to think on my feet, and I give her credit for much of the people motivation that has been so important in my life.

Occasionally I do follow a text line-for-line, but just as often I improvise according to what I feel my audience needs. Thank goodness this ability has provided me with the right answer on a number of occasions when a member of the national media was asking the questions. Let me share just a few personal favorites:

In 1979, "60 Minutes" came calling. After the researchers and producers spent nine days here gathering background, it was time for reporter Morley Safer to interview me. We had been sparring back and forth for a while on a wide range of subjects when Morley suddenly said, "Mary Kay, now I have been around here for a couple of days, and every time I turn around I hear the word God. Aren't you really just using God?" In just a moment I looked him squarely in the eye.

"No, Mr. Safer. I sincerely hope it's the other way around—that God is using me."

On another occasion an extemporaneous speech led to my being on the cover of *The Saturday Evening Post* in 1981. I had spoken to six hundred teachers at the Hershey School in Pennsylvania—ad-libbing from one small notecard what even I acknowledge was a great speech. Unbeknownst to me the editor of the *Post* was in the audience. She followed me to the airport after that speech and pulled a few strings so that she could fly with us to Cleveland for my next speaking engagement that afternoon.

As she sat by me on the plane, she said, "I've made a decision. I want you on the October issue of *The Saturday Evening Post.* By the time I had finished the second speech, the editor had made arrangements for me to be photographed.

One of my favorite quotes came from the cover story in *Savvy* magazine in 1985. I'm sure you know that the media loves to kid us about our pink Cadillacs. The cover of the magazine read, "Mary Kay: So you think pink Cadillacs are tacky? What color was the car your company gave you?" I like that line, and I've used it several times since.

I have also learned to carefully choose my words—most of the time! Recently a member of the media hosted a surprise birthday luncheon for me. As I was getting dressed for the day, I chose to wear a new red suit. When I walked into the party, there was an entire room filled with women, friends, and associates outside Mary Kay—all dressed in pink in my honor. The television news anchor who was hosting the party expressed surprise that I wasn't wearing pink. "Oh," I innocently and glibly remarked, "today I was feeling all pinked out." Well, those very words made the evening news—all the networks plus every major newspaper, asserting that Mary Kay was "all pinked out" and would no longer be having a pink image. Obviously, we still love pink!

In fact, there's a suite named for me at a local hotel, where many of the suites are named for U.S. presidents. Guess what color the decor is? Pink. But when men stay there they call it salmon. Whatever, it works wonderfully for us!

The Right Thing to Do

Remember, I have mentioned that in 1963 my lawyer sent to Washington for a pamphlet telling me how many cosmetic companies went broke every morning? Well, by 1988 the growth rate of Mary Kay Cosmetics was four times greater than the cosmetics industry as a whole. While I was very proud of that phenomenal figure, I think I was even more proud that by 1989, this phenomenal growth was achieved while also taking a stand as a company with an environmental conscience.

As a grandmother of sixteen and a great-grandmother of twenty-five, I feel very strongly that we must do everything in our power to save our planet, or our grandchildren will not have a place to live. Let me emphasize that Mary Kay Cosmetics is an environmental leader because we strongly feel it is the right thing to do.

In 1989 we were one of the first companies to code plastic packaging for recycling. We have provided on-site recycling for our employees since 1989, and since 1991 most of our printed pieces, from my stationery to the four million annual copies of our monthly *Applause* magazine have used recycled paper. Many of our printed pieces use soybean oil–based ink.

We were the first major user of recycled paper stock for four-color printing. Most of our products are packaged in recyclable plastic jars and bottles. Our compacts are refillable and reusable, and we've eliminated cartons and outside packaging wherever it's feasible.

These are some of the innovations that led to Mary Kay Cosmetics being honored with the first United Nations Environment Programme and the Fashion Group International "Fashion and The Environment Award," in addition to being recognized by the United States Environmental Protection Agency.

In 1994 Mary Kay Cosmetics was honored at the World Economic Forum in Switzerland with the Financial Times Television ALP Action Film Award for our recycling video. I am very proud that as a corporation we have set a standard that is truly world-class.

Giving Back

The Bible says, "To whom much is given, much shall be required." And so it is a source of pride to me that we have been able to channel our good fortune toward some very worthy causes. Since my husband Mel died in 1980 with lung cancer, cancer prevention and cancer research have been one of my primary charitable focuses. With 325,000 women in our company now and with the great problem that breast cancer poses, we have redoubled our efforts to try to find a cure through cancer research.

In 1993 I was honored at the dedication of the Mary Kay Ash Center for Cancer Immunotherapy Research at St. Paul Medical Center in Dallas, where the renowned Dr. Amanullah Khan practices. At the St. Paul dedication, the medical center's writers coined a phrase that simultaneously humbled and delighted me. In fact, one of the trade journals named the phrase as "favorite of the year" in the industry. The St. Paul headline reads, "We are named for a saint and endowed by an angel."

I suppose if this "angel" could have one wish it would be that all the cancer researchers in the world would get their heads together and pool their information. Perhaps then we could hasten the time when a cure will be found. Last year, at our Seminar 1993, our beloved Consultants and Directors helped make contributions totaling more than a quarter of a million dollars to our cancer center research. These women reach into their pockets and deep into their hearts for this cause that I hold so dear. In addition to funding, we pray that the new cancer video the company recently completed will give hope and courage to those diagnosed with this terrible disease. We also hope our ongoing public-service program called Skin Wellness can help educate people about sun exposure, skin self-examination, and the warning signs of skin cancer.

In 1993 our employees honored me with the dedication of the Mary Kay Ash/St. Paul Medical Center Mobile Health Screening Unit, which will provide cancer screening at locations throughout Dallas County.

I had another wonderful surprise at our 1993 Seminar, our thirtieth anniversary, when our staff produced in my honor a

"Mary Kay Tribute" at which friends, business associates, employees, and family surprised me onstage with a "This Is Your Life" kind of program. I have never felt so loved. As I told one of our Seminar audiences, "Isn't this, after all, what life is all about? To earn the love and respect of your family, friends, and your co-workers?"

One of the guests at the Tribute was my childhood friend, Dorothy Zapp Brown. Yes, Dorothy is in Chapter 2 in this very book, the person to whom I attribute my competitive spirit! What a joy it was to see her again and for us to instantly resume the friendship that we've enjoyed for so many years. It would be impossible to mention all of the delights of that tribute, but one more I must include.

You remember I talked about the alligator handbag I so desperately wanted to win at that early Stanley convention—and that by the next year they had changed the prize so I did not receive the alligator handbag. I didn't receive it, that is, until Seminar 1993—when the Stanley Corporation sent a member of its board to present me with my very own alligator handbag—three decades later!

The Stanley executive said, "Mary Kay considers this handbag to be the prize that got away. At Stanley, we consider the prize that got away was Mary Kay."

Well, I never considered myself a prize—just an ordinary woman with extraordinary determination.

Whether it was to defy the experts and forge ahead with my dream; or to get out of my hospital bed to keep a date with a national television show that was counting on me; or to patiently smile and make small talk with each of the three thousand women who were waiting to have their photograph made with me, determination and the will to work hard have taken me to places I could once only imagine—and what a beautiful life it has been.

Highlights of Public Appearances, Awards, and Honors

1994

Cover story, *Think & Grow Rich Newsletter,* April issue

Mary Kay Cosmetics listed for the second time on the *Fortune* 500 list, moving up fifty-seven positions in the ranking

Profiled in *Flare,* Canada's premier fashion magazine, February issue

Keynote speaker, *The Dallas Morning News* Distinguished Women Leaders Lecture Series

Featured guest on "Hour of Power" with Dr. Robert Schuller; keynote speaker at Women's Easter Breakfast at the Crystal Cathedral, Garden Grove, California

Financial Times Television ALP Action Award for "Recycling Video"

Profiled in *Hindsight* by Guy Kawasaki

1993

Mary Kay Cosmetics included for the first time on the *Fortune* 500 list of the largest industrial companies in America

Mary Kay Cosmetics listed for the second time in *The 100 Best Companies to Work for in America*

Profiled in *Fortune* magazine feature story, "Mary Kay's Lessons in Leadership," September issue

Featured in *FreEnterprise* cover story, December issue

Dedicated the Mary Kay Museum, a three-thousand-square-foot tribute to thirty years of direct-selling success; Museum featured on CNN and in other national media

Dedicated the Mary Kay Ash Center for Cancer Immunotherapy Research at St. Paul Medical Center, Dallas

Dedicated the Mary Kay Ash/St. Paul Medical Center Mobile Health Screening Unit, Dallas

First female recipient of the Kupfer Distinguished Executive Award, Texas A&M University

Keynote speaker, Seventh Annual Entrepreneurial Woman's Conference in Chicago

Honorary Chairperson, "Midnight at the Meyerson," Dallas Symphony's New Year's Eve Gala

Dallas Mother of the Year Award, Dallas *Can!* Academy

Outstanding Texas Citizen Award, Texas Exchange Clubs

1992

Appeared on "CBS This Morning"

Living Legend Award, Direct Selling Education Foundation

1991

Cover story, the *Chicago Tribune,* Tempo section, February 14

Cited for philanthropic efforts by the Variety Club of Texas

Cover story in *Entrepreneurial Woman,* June 9 issue

Outstanding Woman of the Year, Les Femmes du Monde

1990

Outstanding Business Leader Award, Northwood Institute

National Family Business Award, Baylor University

Women of Achievement Award, General Federation of Women's Clubs

Business Leader of the '90s Award, Association of Woman Business Owners

Individual Komen Award for Philanthropy, Komen Foundation for the Advancement of Breast Cancer Research

1989

Sovereign Fund Award
First Annual National Sales Hall of Fame Award
Circle of Honor Award, Direct Selling Education Foundation

1988

Honorary chairperson, Texas Breast Screening Project
Featured as Outstanding American Businesswoman on a Korean documentary on the United States
Appeared on "Good Morning America" and "CBS This Morning," and featured in "Great American Entrepreneur" series at the Smithsonian Institute

1987

Christian Excellence Award in Business, International Association of Women in Leadership
Positive Approach Award from *A Positive Approach* magazine
Churchwoman of the Year Award, Religious Heritage of America
Profiled in *Woman's Day* magazine on family Thanksgivings

1986

Woman of the Year, Crystal Cathedral Christian Executive Women
Appeared on "Oprah"
Distinguished Woman Award, Northwood Institute
Honored by President Reagan as one of the women entrepreneurs featured in the National Federation of Independent Businesses Report

1985

Ranked eighth in "The Savvy 60" list of top U.S. businesses run by women
Cover story, *Savvy* magazine, June issue
Featured in *People* magazine, July 29 issue

Outstanding Women in Business in Dallas Award, Dallas Chamber of Commerce

Featured in "America's 25 Most Influential Women" from the *World Almanac and Book of Facts*, 1985 edition

1984

Featured in *The 100 Best Companies to Work for in America*

Profiled in *Super Achievers* by Gerhard Gschwandtner

Cover story, the *Robb Report*

Women's Award of Achievement, Women's City Club of Cleveland, Ohio

Mary Kay on People Management published by Warner Books; featured on the *New York Times* best-seller list for eleven weeks

1983

Entrepreneur of the Year Award, Edwin L. Cox School of Business, Southern Methodist University, Dallas, Texas

Appeared on "Good Morning America"

Featured as one of the "100 Most Important Women in America" by *Ladies' Home Journal*

1982

Distinguished Business Leadership Award, University of Texas at Arlington College of Business Administration and Adviser Council

Appeared on "60 Minutes," "Good Morning America," and "Late Night with David Letterman"

Golden Achievement Award from Incentive Manufacturers Representatives Association

Named Outstanding Corporate Sales Executive of 1981 by the *Gallagher Report*, January 4 issue

1981

Business Award for Excellence in Community Service, Dallas Historical Society

Cover story, *The Saturday Evening Post,* October issue
Free Enterprise Award, San Fernando Valley Business and
    Professional Association and the Free Enterprise Award
    Committee
Mary Kay, by Mary Kay, published by Harper & Row
Appeared on "The Today Show," "P.M. Magazine," and "Phil
    Donahue"

1980
Golden Plate Award, American Academy of Achievement
Appeared on "To Tell the Truth" television game show

1979
Profiled on "60 Minutes"
Appeared on "The 700 Club"

1978
Horatio Alger Distinguished American Citizen Award, Horatio
    Alger Association
Cosmetic Career Woman of the Year Award
Dale Carnegie Leadership Award